AS/A2 STUDENT GUIDE

CCEA

Physics

Unit 3 Practical techniques and data analysis

Roy White

This Guide has been written specifically to support students preparing for the CCEA AS/A-level Physics Unit 3 examinations. The content has been neither approved nor endorsed by CCEA and remains the sole responsibility of the author.

Although every effort has been made to ensure that website addresses are correct at time of going to press, Hodder Education cannot be held responsible for the content of any website mentioned in this book. It is sometimes possible to find a relocated web page by typing in the address of the home page for a website in the URL window of your browser.

Hachette UK's policy is to use papers that are natural, renewable and recyclable products and made from wood grown in well-managed forests and other controlled sources. The logging and manufacturing processes are expected to conform to the environmental regulations of the country of origin.

Orders: please contact Hachette UK Distribution, Hely Hutchinson Centre, Milton Road, Didcot, Oxfordshire, OX11 7HH. Telephone: +44 (0)1235 827827. Email education@hachette.co.uk Lines are open from 9 a.m. to 5 p.m., Monday to Friday.
You can also order through our website: www.hoddereducation.com

© Roy White 2020

ISBN 978-1-5104-8609-6

First printed 2020

First published in 2020 by
Hodder Education,
An Hachette UK Company
Carmelite House
50 Victoria Embankment
London EC4Y 0DZ

www.hoddereducation.co.uk

The authorised representative in the EEA is Hachette Ireland, 8 Castlecourt Centre, Dublin 15, D15 XTP3, Ireland (email: info@hbgi.ie)

Impression number 10 9 8 7 6 5 4 3 2

Year 2024 2023

All rights reserved. Apart from any use permitted under UK copyright law, no part of this publication may be reproduced or transmitted in any form or by any means, electronic or mechanical, including photocopying and recording, or held within any information storage and retrieval system, without permission in writing from the publisher or under licence from the Copyright Licensing Agency Limited. Further details of such licences (for reprographic reproduction) may be obtained from the Copyright Licensing Agency Limited, www.cla.co.uk.

Cover photo: kasiastock/Fotolia

Typeset in India by Aptara Inc.

Printed and bound by CPI Group (UK) Ltd, Croydon, CR0 4YY

A catalogue record for this title is available from the British Library.

Contents

Getting the most from this book 5
About this book 6

Content Guidance

Mathematical content 7
    Arithmetic and numerical computation • Handling data
    • Algebra • Graphs • Geometry and trigonometry

Practical skills 23
    Implementing • Analysis • Evaluation • Refinement
    • Communication

Practical activities 1–23 32
  1 Determine the density of a solid or liquid 33
  2 Determine (a) the value of an unknown mass and (b) the mass of
     a uniform ruler using the principle of moments 35
  3 Determine the acceleration of free fall by means of a falling
     object and light gates 38
  4 Verification of the mathematical form of Newton's second law .. 41
  5 Verification of the conservation of linear momentum in a collision .. 44
  6 Investigate the energy exchange between potential and kinetic
     for a falling body 46
  7 Determine resistance by the ammeter–voltmeter method and using
     a multimeter or ohmmeter and the I–V characteristics of a metallic
     conductor at constant temperature and a filament lamp 48
  8 Verify the relationships for resistors in (a) series and (b) parallel 51
  9 Determine the resistivity of a material 53
 10 Determine the resistance–temperature characteristic of a negative
    temperature coefficient (ntc) thermistor 55
 11 Determine the e.m.f. and internal resistance of a battery 58
 12 Verify Snell's law and determine the refractive index of a material ... 60
 13 Determine the critical angle of glass or Perspex® using a
    semicircular block 63
 14 Determine the focal length of a converging lens and verify
    experimentally the lens equation for real images 64

Contents

15 Verify that the magnification of a real image is equal to the ratio of the image distance to the object distance 66

16 Determine the speed of sound in air using a resonance tube 69

17 Determine the wavelength of light using a double slit 71

18 Determine the wavelength of light using a diffraction grating 73

19 Determine the Young modulus for the material of a metal wire 76

20 Perform and describe an electrical method for determining specific heat capacity (of a liquid).. 78

21 Investigate experimentally the motion of the simple pendulum and the loaded spiral spring 80

22 Describe experiments to demonstrate the discharge and charge of a capacitor and measure the time constant 84

23 Describe how the cathode ray oscilloscope (CRO) can be used to determine the voltage and frequency 88

Questions & Answers

About this section 90
AS 3B paper-style questions..................................... 92
A2 3B paper-style questions..................................... 100

Knowledge check answers 105
Index 107

Getting the most from this book

Exam tips
Advice on key points in the text to help you learn and recall content, avoid pitfalls, and polish your exam technique in order to boost your grade.

Knowledge check
Rapid-fire questions throughout the Content Guidance section to check your understanding.

Knowledge check answers
1 Turn to the back of the book for the Knowledge check answers.

Exam-style questions

Commentary on the questions
Tips on what you need to do to gain full marks.

Sample student answers
Practise the questions, then look at the student answers that follow.

Commentary on sample student answers
Read the comments showing how many marks each answer would be awarded in the exam and exactly where marks are gained or lost.

About this book

This student guide covers the practical assessment for the CCEA specifications for AS and A2 physics. It offers advice for the effective development of practical skills. It is not intended as a replacement for carrying out practical work. The guide has four sections:

- Mathematical content
- Practical skills
- Practical activities
- Questions & Answers

The **Mathematical content** section incorporates the mathematical skills that you need for the AS and A2 examination, together with a reminder of the importance of units. For A2, you need the advanced mathematical skills highlighted in bold type.

This section provides the basis of all calculations that you will be required to undertake. Without these mathematical skills, you will not be able to analyse your data and subsequently draw conclusions about your experiment. You are advised to work through this section and put your knowledge to the test by attempting the questions as you go along.

The **Practical skills** section identifies the essential skills needed for successful practical work, based on the practical criteria set out in the specification. It will help you become a confident practical physicist, able to use a variety of apparatus and techniques to collect data, which can then be analysed and used to draw valid conclusions.

The **Practical activities** section reflects the CCEA requirement that you should acquire competence and confidence in a variety of practical, mathematical and problem-solving skills and in handling apparatus competently and safely. Each of the activities is discussed in detail, focusing on one practical identified in the specification, with worked examples based on experimental data.

You should remember also that the knowledge, understanding and skills on which you will be assessed in Unit 3A are exactly the same as those that you will have met when carrying out practical activities referred to in the specification. It is for that reason that these practicals are all covered in this section.

The **Questions & Answers** section pulls together the other three sections through a range of practice questions based on the type of question that will be asked in examination papers to test practical knowledge, particularly in Unit 3B. It does not in itself replicate a complete examination paper, as it contains only questions that test practical skills. Answers are provided, and common errors made by students are also highlighted so that you, hopefully, do not make the same mistakes.

The key to doing well in any examination is preparation. The knowledge check questions are there to encourage you to reflect on your learning and to reinforce the ideas and concepts you are encountering in your course. Do study the worked examples and attempt all the questions. They are there to show you good practice and are pitched at the level you can expect in your exam. After doing each question, check your answer with that given later in the book. If you have made an error, learn from your mistake, so that you are less likely to make the same slip in the exam.

A-level physics is a course that demands much of the student. It is challenging and rigorous and it makes you think. But it is also fun. I wish you well in your studies.

Content Guidance

■ Mathematical content

To do well in AS or A2 physics, you will need to be familiar with the units in which physics measurements are made and how they are combined mathematically. Perhaps more than in any other GCE science, the development of your mathematical skills in physics is vital if you are to achieve the highest grades.

The mathematical material with which you are expected to be familiar is identified in Appendix 1 of the specification. It is worth examining it closely, particularly as you prepare for your AS and A2 examinations. This chapter will help you to focus on how these skills are used in your practical work.

Arithmetic and numerical computation

Throughout your studies you will need to:
- recognise and make use of appropriate units in calculations
- recognise and use expressions in decimal and standard form
- use ratios, fractions and percentages
- estimate results
- use calculators to find and use power functions, exponential and logarithmic functions
- use calculators to handle $\sin x$, $\cos x$ and $\tan x$ when x is expressed in degrees or radians

Physicists use the **SI system** (Système Internationale) of measurement. This system is based on seven fundamental **base units**, of which you are required to know the six shown in Table 1.

Table 1 SI base units

Measurement	Unit	Abbreviation
Mass	kilogram	kg
Length	metre	m
Time	second	s
Current	ampere	A
Temperature	kelvin	K
Amount of substance	mole	mol

SI system The international system of units adopted worldwide by the physics community.

Base units The units on which the SI system is based.

Content Guidance

All other SI units are combinations of the base units and are called **derived units**. Some of the more common derived units are listed in Table 2.

Table 2 Common derived units in A-level physics

Physical quantity	Common unit	Abbreviation	Derived unit
Area	square metres	m²	m²
Volume	cubic metres	m³	m³
Density	kilogram per cubic metre	kg m⁻³	kg m⁻³
Pressure	pascal	Pa	kg m⁻¹ s⁻²
Specific heat capacity	joule per kilogram per kelvin	J kg⁻¹ K⁻¹	m² s⁻² K⁻¹
Speed	metre per second	m s⁻¹	m s⁻¹
Energy	joule	J	kg m² s⁻²
Force	newton	N	kg m s⁻²
Gravitational field strength	newton per kilogram	N kg⁻¹	m s⁻²
Acceleration	metre per squared second	m s⁻²	m s⁻²
Power	watt	W	kg m² s⁻³
Frequency	hertz	Hz	s⁻¹
Electric charge	coulomb	C	A s
Electrical potential difference	volt	V	kg A⁻¹ m² s⁻³
Electrical resistance	ohm	Ω	kg A⁻² m² s⁻³
Magnetic flux density	tesla	T	kg A⁻¹ s⁻²

> **Derived units** Combinations of SI base units.
>
> **Knowledge check 1**
> State the derived unit in which you would measure the following physical quantities: (a) resistivity, (b) stress, (c) strain, (d) Young modulus.

Decimal and standard form

Physicists measure quantities as large as the size of the universe and as small as the mass of an electron. Prefixes are used for very small or very large measurements. Table 3 gives some of the common prefixes used in physics.

Table 3 **Submultiple** and **multiple** units in A-level physics

Submultiples		Multiples	
Prefix and symbol	Factor of 10	Prefix and symbol	Factor of 10
centi, c	10^{-2}		
milli, m	10^{-3}	kilo, k	10^3
micro, μ	10^{-6}	mega, M	10^6
nano, n	10^{-9}	giga, G	10^9
pico, p	10^{-12}	tera, T	10^{12}
femto, f	10^{-15}		

It is sometimes necessary to change from one unit to another. For example, the density of ethanol is 790 kg m⁻³. What is that in g cm⁻³? To answer this question, we must convert kg to g and m³ to cm³. Now 1 kg is 1000 g and 1 m³ is (100 cm × 100 cm × 100 cm) or 1 000 000 cm³. So 1 kg m⁻³ = 1000 g/(1 000 000) cm³ = 0.001 g cm⁻³.

Hence 790 kg m⁻³ = (790 × 0.001) g cm⁻³ = 0.79 g cm⁻³.

> **Standard form** A number in the form $a \times 10^n$, where n is a whole number and $1 \leq a < 10$.
>
> **Submultiples** Fractions of a base unit or a derived unit.
>
> **Multiples** Large numbers of a base unit or a derived unit.
>
> **Knowledge check 2**
> The radius of the hydrogen atom is about 53 pm and the electron orbiting its nucleus does so at a speed of about 22 Mm s⁻¹. Express these values in m and m s⁻¹ in **standard form**.

Mathematical content

Ratios, fractions and percentages

The use of ratios, fractions and percentages is no more demanding in A-level physics than you experienced in GCSE mathematics. However, it is worth looking at the knowledge checks opposite to confirm your understanding.

Trigonometrical ratios

These are the familiar $\sin x$, $\cos x$ and $\tan x$. At AS, you first come across them in resolving and adding vectors. At A2, you meet them at various parts of the course, but especially when dealing with refraction and diffraction.

A2 students are expected to be familiar with the use of radians as a measure of angles. While it is important to know that the conversion formula from radians to degrees is π radians = 180 degrees, it is essential that you are familiar with the operation of your calculator in both measures. Most scientific calculators allow you to select the unit required using the <Shift> <Mode> buttons.

> **Exam tip**
> Always check whether the values you are given in an exam question have prefixes. Convert these into standard form before you attempt to answer the question.

> **Knowledge check 3**
> A metal alloy is made of iron, manganese and chromium in the ratio 7:2:1.
> a What fraction of the alloy is made of chromium?
> b What percentage of the alloy is made of non-ferrous metals?
> c What is the ratio of iron:other metals?

Worked example

The angle of refraction in a square block of glass of side 20 cm and refractive index 1.50 is 19°. Calculate **a** the angle of incidence and **b** the length of the path taken by the ray of light in the glass.

Answer

a From Snell's law, $r = \sin^{-1}(n \times \sin r) = \sin^{-1}(1.5 \times \sin 19) = \sin^{-1}(0.488) = 29.2°$

b $D = \dfrac{\text{length of square}}{\cos r} = \dfrac{20}{\cos 19} = 21.2 \text{ cm}$

Exponentials and natural logarithms

AS students do not usually have to use exponentials and natural logarithms. At A2, exponentials and logarithms are mainly found in the topics of capacitance and radioactivity. Exponential growth occurs when the variable you are measuring increases by the same proportion in each equal interval of time. Exponential decay occurs when the measured variable decreases by the same proportion in each equal interval of time.

> **Knowledge check 4**
> The refractive index of a material is the ratio of the speed of light in air to the speed of light in that material. If the refractive index of glass is 1.50 and the refractive index of water is 1.33, calculate the ratio speed of light in water:speed of light in glass.

Worked example

(**A2 only**) The activity of a radioisotope falls from 1200 Bq to 800 Bq in 40 minutes. Find the decay constant and the half-life of the radioisotope.

Answer

From the law of radioactive decay: $A = A_0 e^{-\lambda t}$

Taking natural logs of both sides: $\ln A = \ln A_0 - \lambda t$

Rearranging: $\lambda = \dfrac{\ln A_0 - \ln A}{t}$

> **Knowledge check 5**
> Find the angle for which tan is 1.500, giving your answer in degrees and in radians.

Content Guidance

Substituting: $\lambda = \dfrac{\ln 1200 - \ln 800}{40}$

$\lambda = 10.137 \times 10^{-3}\,\text{min}^{-1}$

From half-life equation:

$T_{\frac{1}{2}} = \dfrac{0.693}{\lambda}$

$T_{\frac{1}{2}} = \dfrac{0.693}{10.137 \times 10^{-3}}$

$T_{\frac{1}{2}} = 68.4\,\text{minutes}$

> **Exam tip**
>
> A-level students have about 2 years to learn their way around a calculator. Get to know it well. Do not buy a calculator with which you are not familiar a few weeks before your exam.

Handling data

Throughout your studies you will need to:
- make order-of-magnitude calculations
- use an appropriate number of significant figures (sf)
- find arithmetic means

Estimation and orders of magnitude

Part of the skill set of an experimental physicist is the ability to make estimates. Physicists sometimes talk about an estimate 'to within an order of magnitude'. The order of magnitude is the **index** when a quantity is expressed in standard form. The charge on an electron is $1.6 \times 10^{-19}\,\text{C}$. So, the order of magnitude is 10^{-19}. When physicists refer to 'within an order of magnitude for the electron charge', they mean between $10^{-18}\,\text{C}$ and $10^{-20}\,\text{C}$.

Index The power to which a number or letter is raised. The plural of index is indices.

The key to making estimates is to work to 1 or 2 significant figures only. For example, the volume of a typical school laboratory is about $10\,\text{m} \times 10\,\text{m} \times 3\,\text{m}$ or $300\,\text{m}^3$. It is a good approximation to take π as 3 or 3.1.

> **Worked example**
>
> Estimate the density of steel.
>
> **Answer**
>
> We already know that the density will be greater than $1\,\text{g}\,\text{cm}^{-3}$ because a steel ball bearing will sink in water.
>
> From experience a small steel ball bearing has a mass of about $5\,\text{g}$ (this estimate means its mass lies between $0.5\,\text{g}$ and $50\,\text{g}$ — correct to within an order of magnitude).
>
> Its radius is certainly less than $1\,\text{cm}$, say $0.5\,\text{cm}$.
>
> So its volume = $\dfrac{4}{3} \times \pi r^3 \sim \dfrac{\pi}{6}$ or $0.5\,\text{cm}^3$.
>
> Its density is therefore about $\dfrac{5\,\text{g}}{0.5\,\text{cm}^3}$, which is around $10\,\text{g}\,\text{cm}^{-3}$.
>
> This compares well with the actual density of steel, which is around $8\,\text{g}\,\text{cm}^{-3}$.

Mathematical content

Significant figures

Significant figures are the figures in a number that are meaningful or useful. When doing a practical, the number of significant figures recorded in your data will depend on the precision of the equipment you are using.

Giving the correct number of significant figures in calculations is important because it signifies the degree of precision.

Suppose we measure a mass on a balance capable of reading to the nearest 10 g and we get a reading of 5170 g. This tells us the mass (M) can be estimated as 5165 g $\leq M <$ 5175 g. For all masses between 1000 g and 9990 g this balance would give us a reading to 3 sf (the 5, 1 and 7), and the units digit would always be zero.

Worked example

A trolley of mass 585 g has an acceleration down a runway of 24 cm s^{-2}. Calculate the size of the resultant force.

Answer

$$F = ma = 0.585 \text{ kg} \times 0.24 \text{ m s}^{-2} = 0.1404 \text{ N}$$

The data in the question are given to 2 sf and 3 sf. The answer should therefore be given to just 2 sf. In this case, the answer should be given as 0.14 N.

Arithmetic mean

The arithmetic **mean** is simply the value obtained by dividing the sum of a set of terms by the number of terms. Means are used extensively in practical physics to reduce random error. For example, if four different measurements of a given mass are 65 g, 66 g, 64 g and 65 g, then their mean value is (65 + 66 + 64 + 65)/4 = 65 g.

Algebra

A working knowledge of basic algebra and an ability to manipulate equations are essential tools for A-level physics students.

Throughout your studies you will need to:
- understand and use the symbols =, <, <<, >>, >, ∝ and ≈
- change the subject of an equation
- substitute numerical values into algebraic equations using appropriate units for physical quantities
- solve simple algebraic equations

Symbols

Symbols are a useful shorthand to express mathematical relationships. You will probably be familiar with those given in Table 4 from your earlier studies in mathematics.

Significant figures (sf) Approximations to a number determined by a set of mathematical rules.

Exam tip

In general, when you are doing a calculation, the number of significant figures in the answer should be the same as that number with the minimum number of sf in the question. This means that intermediate numbers should always be to a higher number of sf.

Exam tip

You can often check in your head whether your answer to a calculation is reasonable by converting all the numbers to 1 sf and carrying out the necessary mental arithmetic.

Knowledge check 6

A current of 34 mA flows through a conductor when the voltage across it is 2.55 V. Calculate the resistance of the wire, giving your answer to an appropriate number of significant figures.

Knowledge check 7

Can you think of any four-digit number which is the same to 1, 2, 3 or 4 significant figures?

Mean (sometimes referred to as the arithmetic mean) The sum of a set of values divided by the number of values in the set. It is frequently called the average.

Practical techniques and data analysis

Content Guidance

Table 4 Required mathematical symbols

Symbol	Meaning
<	is less than
<<	is much less than
>	is greater than
>>	is much greater than
∝	is directly proportional to
≈	is approximately equal to

Sometimes these symbols are put together. For example, $5 < S < 10$ means that '5 is less than S, **and** S is less than 10'. This is just a short way of writing S lies between 5 and 10, but is not equal to either 5 or 10.

Changing the subject of an equation

Almost all physics definitions and physical laws can be reduced to an algebraic equation. You can immediately think of the definitions for density, pressure, uniform acceleration and so on. The letter to the immediate left of the equals sign is called the subject. For example, one of the energy equations with which you are familiar is $E_k = \tfrac{1}{2}mv^2$. In this equation, E_k is the subject. If you need to calculate E_k, substitute numbers for m and v and carry out the arithmetic on a calculator (if necessary).

Suppose you know E_k and m, but you need to find v. Then you need to make v the subject of the equation. The worked example shows how you might do this.

> **Knowledge check 8**
>
> Write the following statements as equations using the appropriate mathematical symbols:
>
> a The angle of incidence in air is greater than the angle of refraction in glass.
>
> b The mass of an electron is very much less than the mass of a proton.
>
> c The speed of a photon in air is approximately equal to that of light in a vacuum.

Worked example

The kinetic energy of a proton of mass 1.66×10^{-27} kg is 5.312×10^{-20} J. Calculate its speed in km s^{-1}.

Answer

From the definition of kinetic energy: $E_k = \tfrac{1}{2}mv^2$

Multiply both sides of the equation by 2: $2E_k = 2 \times \left(\tfrac{1}{2}mv^2\right) = mv^2$

Divide both sides of the equation by m: $\dfrac{2E_k}{m} = \dfrac{mv^2}{m}$

Cancel m on the right-hand side: $\dfrac{2E_k}{m} = v^2$

Take the square root of both sides of the equation: $\left(\dfrac{2E_k}{m}\right)^{\tfrac{1}{2}} = v$

Make v the subject: $v = \left(\dfrac{2E_k}{m}\right)^{\tfrac{1}{2}}$

Make the substitutions for E_k and m: $v = \sqrt{(2 \times 5.312 \times 10^{-20})/1.66 \times 10^{-27}}$

Use a calculator to carry out the arithmetic: $v = 8000$ m s^{-1}

Convert to the correct unit (km s^{-1}): $v = 8.00$ km s^{-1}

Note that the answer is given to 3 sf because the numbers in the question were to 3 sf and 4 sf.

> **Exam tip**
>
> Always show your full working for calculations. By doing so you may pick up marks for a correct method even if your final answer is incorrect.

Mathematical content

Knowledge check 9

Rearrange the following equations so that the quantity shown in square brackets after each equation is the subject of the rearranged equation.

$P = \dfrac{F}{A}$ [A]

$T = k\left(\dfrac{L}{g}\right)^{\frac{1}{2}}$ [g]

$E = V + IR$ [R]

$y = \lambda \dfrac{D}{a}$ [λ]

$v^2 = \omega^2(A^2 - x^2)$ [x]

> **Exam tip**
>
> If, in numerical problems, you find equations are too time-consuming to rearrange, make the substitutions immediately and then you have only numbers and the unknown letter to work with. But be aware that there are situations, such as mapping an equation to that for a straight line, where there is no alternative but to rearrange. This topic is dealt with in the next section on graphs.

Graphs

Physics is all about relationships between quantities that can be measured. To find such relationships, graphs are an invaluable tool. They allow us to see visually a relationship that is much more difficult to see simply by looking at the numbers in a table.

Throughout your course you will need to:

- translate information between graphical, numerical and algebraic forms
- plot two variables from experimental or other data
- understand that $y = mx + c$ represents a linear relationship
- determine the slope and intercept of a linear graph
- draw and use the slope of a tangent to a curve as a measure of rate of change
- understand the possible physical significance of the area between a curve and the x-axis, and be able to calculate it or measure it by counting squares, as appropriate
- **use logarithmic plots to test exponential and power law variations**
- sketch simple functions including:

$y = \dfrac{k}{x}$, $y = kx^2$, $y = \dfrac{k}{x^2}$, $y = \sin x$, $y = \cos x$ and $y = e^{-x}$

> **Exam tip**
>
> In physics it is customary to plot the dependent variable on the y-axis and the independent variable on the x-axis. But that is not always the case. There is no rigid rule. For example, it is usual to plot time on the x-axis, irrespective of whether it is the dependent or independent variable. You need to look carefully at the axes and ask yourself what message is being conveyed by the graph.

Straight-line graphs

All straight-line graphs have the form $y = mx + c$, where m is the gradient of the graph (sometimes called the slope) and c is a constant. Notice from the equation $y = mx + c$ that, when $x = 0$, the value of y is equal to c. This tells us that the coordinates of the point where the graph crosses the y-axis are $(0, c)$. The point $(0, c)$ is called the y-axis intercept. Often this is simply written 'c is the intercept'.

If a straight-line graph also goes through the origin, it demonstrates direct proportion. You will have come across many such graphs in your study of physics. Examples include extension and force for a spring (Hooke's law), current and voltage for a metal wire at constant temperature (Ohm's law), resultant force and acceleration for a moving object (Newton's second law). The list is almost endless.

Practical techniques and data analysis

Content Guidance

Often the goal of practical physics is to rearrange the equation describing the relationship into linear form. Such rearrangements are called 'mapping to a linear form'. Being able to carry out such transformations is an essential skill for the experimental physicist.

> **Worked example**
>
> Inspect the graphs in Figure 1 and then state, with a reason:
> a which show a linear relationship
> b which show direct proportion
>
>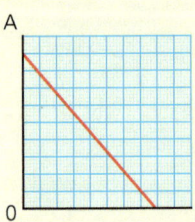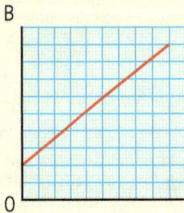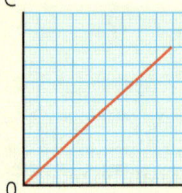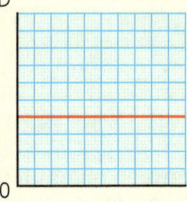
>
> **Figure 1** Straight line graphs
>
> **Answer**
> a All are straight lines, so all show a linear relationship.
> b Only C shows a straight line through the origin, so only C shows direct proportion.

> **Exam tip**
>
> Choose scales on each axis with care. Usually there are 5 or 10 small squares between each of the main grid lines. Choosing 5 or 10 small squares to represent 1, 2, 4, 5 or 10 units is fine. Choosing it to mean 3 units is not because it makes interpolation difficult, for example when working out the meaning of 7 small squares. The issue is important because examiners will penalise the choice of an inappropriate scale.

Simple mappings

You will be aware that an object starting from rest with an acceleration a reaches a speed v after travelling a distance S. The equation describing this motion is:

$$v^2 = 2aS$$

If you were to plot experimentally determined values of v against S, the graph you would obtain is a curve of decreasing gradient that passes through the origin. The relationship is non-linear. However, with a suitable mapping, you could obtain a straight-line graph.

Consider what the graph of v^2 against S would look like by mapping directly to $y = mx + c$.

$$v^2 = 2a\,\mathbf{S}$$
$$y\ = m\mathbf{x} + c$$

We are plotting: v^2 on the vertical axis, so v^2 corresponds to y

S on the horizontal axis, so S corresponds to x

Comparing shows $2a$ corresponds to the gradient.

Mathematical content

There is nothing that corresponds to c, so the graph of v^2 against S passes through $(0, 0)$ (Figure 2).

We have now mapped the quadratic equation to a linear form.

A graph of v against S shows a curve, but a graph of v^2 against S is a straight line through $(0, 0)$.

However, this linear graph is now very useful.
- If we measure the gradient and halve it, we have found the acceleration a. To find the acceleration is much more difficult with a curve.
- We have also demonstrated that v^2 is **directly proportional** to S.

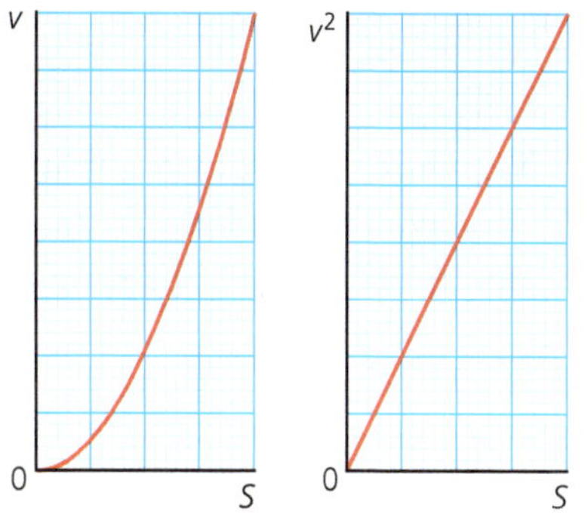

Figure 2 Motion graphs

Measuring the gradient

To measure the gradient of a straight-line graph:
- Draw a large right-angled triangle using the part of the line of best fit as the hypotenuse.
- Determine the rise (on the vertical axis) and the run on the horizontal axis, by reading and subtracting the relevant numbers on each.
- Calculate the gradient as the ratio rise/run.
- Determine the unit by dividing the unit on the y-axis by the unit on the x-axis.

This process is illustrated in Figure 3.

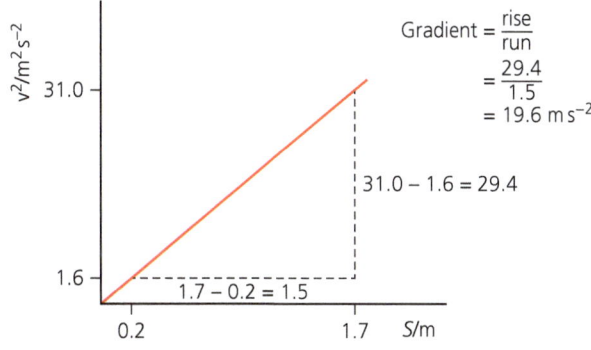

Figure 3 Finding the gradient of a straight-line graph

To measure the gradient of a curve:

The gradient of a curve changes at every point along its path. The first task therefore is to select the point of interest and, using a ruler, draw a tangent there. We then find the gradient of this straight-line tangent. Drawing the tangent is illustrated in Figure 4.

Significance of the gradient

The gradient of a graph always represents a rate of change. The gradient of the curve in Figure 4 represents the rate of change of velocity with time, that is, acceleration. The horizontal axis need not always be time. For example, the gradient of the graph of resistance against current for a thermistor is the rate of change of resistance with current.

Directly proportional
Quantities are in a constant ratio.

Knowledge check 10

The terminal voltage across a battery, V, is related to the current drawn from it, I, according to the equation $E = V + rI$, where E is the e.m.f. of the battery and r is its internal resistance. Both E and r are constants.

a What straight-line graph could a student plot in order to verify this relationship?

b How could E and r be found from this graph?

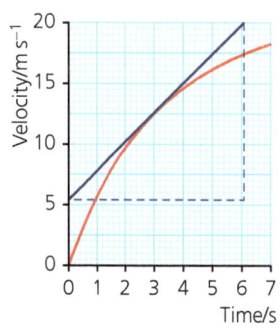

Figure 4 Finding the gradient at a point on a curve

Content Guidance

> **Worked example**
>
> A student measures the activity A of a short half-life radioisotope as it decays over time.
> **a** Map the decay equation to that for a straight line.
> **b** What does the student have to plot to obtain a straight-line graph?
> **c** How might the student determine from this the decay constant λ and half-life of the radioisotope $T_{1/2}$?
> **d** What is represented by the intercept of the graph?
>
> **Answer**
>
> **a** The decay equation is:
> $$A = A_0 e^{-\lambda t}$$
> Taking natural logs: $\ln A = \ln A_0 - \lambda t$ which maps to $y = c + mx$.
> **b** Plotting $\ln A$ against t will give a straight-line graph.
> **c** The gradient of the graph of $\ln A$ against t is $-\lambda$.
> The half-life is the value of $\dfrac{0.693}{\lambda}$.
> **d** The intercept is $\ln A_0$, where A_0 is the activity at time $t = 0$.

> **Knowledge check 11**
>
> **a** Show that the gradient of the curve in Figure 4 is approximately $2.4\,\text{m}\,\text{s}^{-2}$.
> **b** State whether the gradient of this curve is increasing or decreasing as time increases.

> **Exam tip**
>
> The graph of any exponential function in the form $y = Ae^{kx}$ is always a curve for any non-zero value of k. To find A and k, plot the graph of $\ln y$ against x and draw the straight line of best fit. Then A is $e^{\text{intercept}}$ and k is the gradient.

Area under graphs

In some graphs, the area between the graph and the horizontal axis is of great interest. For example, the area between the velocity–time graph and the horizontal axis represents the displacement, and the area between the force–extension graph and the horizontal axis represents the work done.

Finding the area is easily done if the graph is a straight line or a series of straight lines, by dividing the space between the graph and the horizontal axis into triangles and squares. The unit for the area is the product of the units on the vertical and horizontal axes.

Part of the mathematical requirement for AS and A2 is that you can calculate the area under a curve, not just a straight line. To calculate the area under a curve you have to count squares.

> **Worked example**
>
> The curve in Figure 5 shows how the velocity of an aircraft changes as it accelerates down a runway prior to take-off. Find the displacement of the aircraft after 9 seconds.

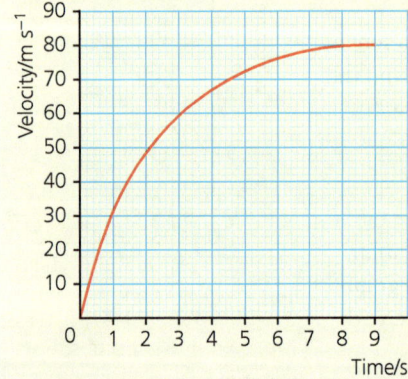

Figure 5 Velocity–time graph showing decreasing acceleration

Mathematical content

Answer

Each of the large squares on the grid represents an area of $10\,\mathrm{m\,s^{-1}} \times 1\,\mathrm{s}$ or $10\,\mathrm{m}$.

The area between a velocity–time graph and the time axis represents the displacement.

To find this area, we count squares. Where the area is less than half a square, it is ignored. Where the area is more than half a square, it is regarded as a full square.

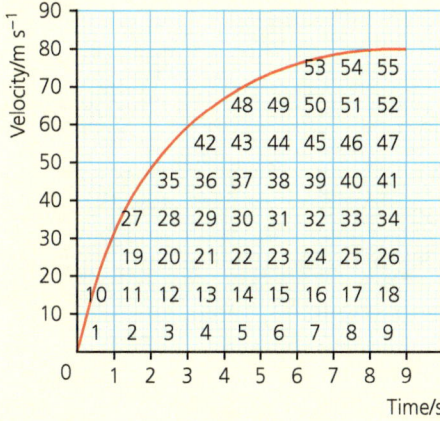

Figure 6 Finding displacement from a velocity–time graph

There are 55 such squares shown on the graph in Figure 6, so the total displacement is $55 \times 10\,\mathrm{m} = 550\,\mathrm{m}$.

Logarithmic plots

Sometimes physics students are asked to confirm that the relationship between variables is of the form $y = kx^n$. This is straightforward if n is known — a graph of y against x^n is a straight line through the origin of gradient k. If the value of n is not known, then an approach using logs is required. What graph should you plot? (Be aware that such activity only arises in A2, not AS.)

Suppose the periodic time of an oscillation T is thought to be related to a quantity r by the equation:

$T = kr^n$

where k and n are unknown constants.

Then, by the theory of logarithms, $\log T = \log k + n \times \log r$.

We can map this to the equation of a straight line, $y = c + mx$, where: $\log T$ corresponds to y, $\log k$ corresponds to c, n corresponds to the gradient m and $\log r$ corresponds to x.

Worked example

In a mathematical model of a planetary system, T represents the period in years of planets travelling around a star and r represents the average distance between the planet and the star in Gm.

Content Guidance

T in Ms	32	91	166	256	358
r in Gm	150	300	450	600	750

It is thought that T is related to a quantity r by the equation $T = kr^n$, where k and n are unknown constants. By plotting a suitable linear graph, determine the numerical values of k and n, giving your answers to 2 sf.

Answer

Taking logs gives:

$$\log T = \log k + n \times \log r$$

T/Ms	32	91	166	256	316
r/Gm	150	300	450	600	750
log(T/Ms)	1.51	1.96	2.22	2.41	2.50
log(r/Gm)	2.18	2.48	2.65	2.78	2.88

The graph of $\log T$ against $\log r$ is a straight line of gradient n and intercept $\log k$ (Figure 7).

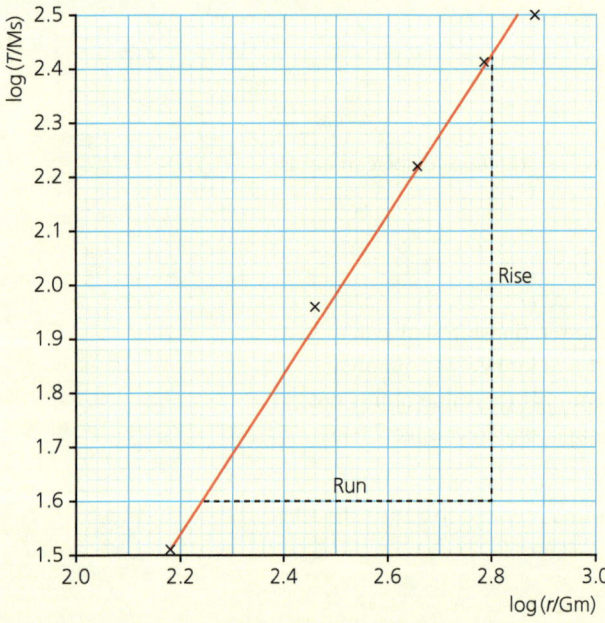

Figure 7 Graph of $\log T$ against $\log r$ for planets

n = gradient = rise/run = $(2.41 - 1.60)/(2.80 - 2.24) = 1.45$ (3 sf)
equation of line is $\log T = 1.45 \log r - 1.65$

$\log k$ = intercept $c = -1.65$, so $k = 10^{-1.65} = 0.022$ (2 sf)
(A2 students will recognise these ideas from Kepler's third law.)

If the suspected physical relationship involves the base of natural logarithms e, then the logs are taken to base e and are written $\ln$ instead of $\log$, that is, $\ln x = \log_e x$.

For example, if it is suspected that the intensity of gamma rays I depends on the thickness x of a lead absorber according to the equation:

$$I = I_0 e^{-kx}$$

then taking natural logs of both sides gives:

$\ln I = \ln I_0 - kx$

and a graph of $\ln I$ against x would be a straight line of gradient $-k$ and intercept $\ln I_0$.

> **Knowledge check 12**
>
> Without using a calculator, state the value of $\ln(e^{-10})$.

Sketching simple functions

Graphs of various functions that you are likely to encounter at various points in your course are shown in Figure 8.

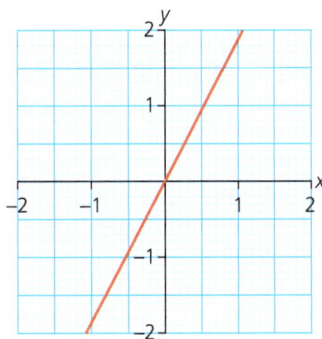

(a) Graph of $y = kx$, where k is a constant

Graph of $y = mx$, where m is a constant equal to the gradient.

This graph shows that y is directly proportional to x.

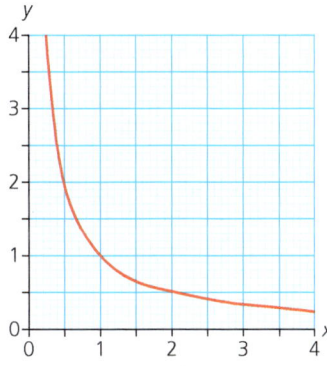

(b) Graph of $y = \dfrac{k}{x}$, where k is a constant

Graph of $y = k/x$, where k is a constant.

This is the graph obtained if y is inversely proportional to x. To obtain a straight-line graph in such a situation, plot y against $1/x$.

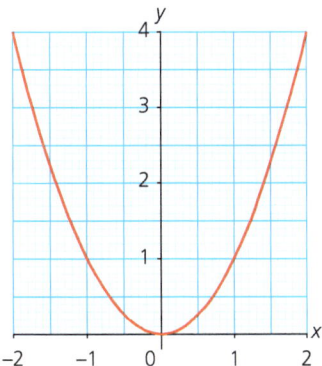

(c) Graph of $y = kx^2$, where k is a constant, in this case $k = 1$

Graph of $y = kx^2$, where k is a constant, in this case $k = 1$.

This is the shape of the graph obtained if y is the kinetic energy of a moving object and v is the velocity. To obtain a straight-line graph in such a situation, plot y against x^2.

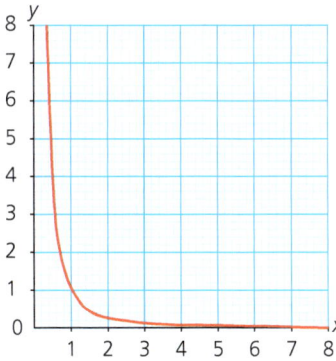

(d) Graph of $y = \dfrac{k}{x^2}$, where k is a constant, in this case $k = 1$

Graph of $y = k/x^2$, where k is a constant.

This is the graph obtained if y is inversely proportional to x^2. To obtain a straight-line graph in such a situation, plot y against $1/x^2$

Figure 8 Miscellaneous graphs (continued on the next page)

Content Guidance

The following are graphs of various exponential and trigonometrical functions.

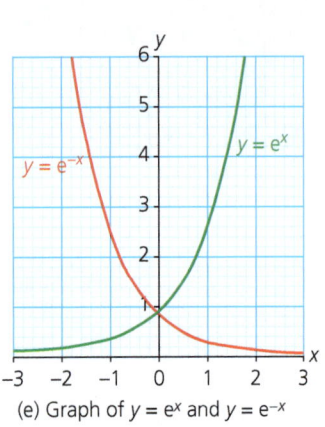
(e) Graph of $y = e^x$ and $y = e^{-x}$

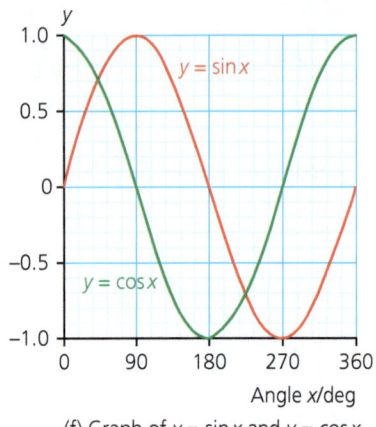
(f) Graph of $y = \sin x$ and $y = \cos x$

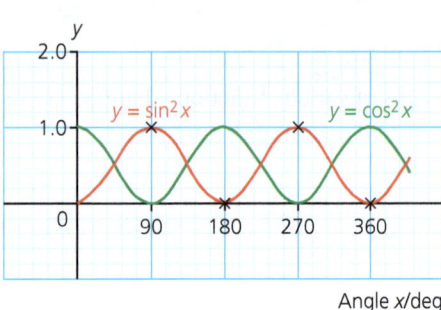
(g) Graph of $y = \sin^2 x$ and $y = \cos^2 x$

Figure 8 (continued)

Geometry and trigonometry

Physicists often use models to describe and explain the real world. The globe hanging from a ceiling in a classroom, for example, is a model of the Earth. Often, however, the models used by physicists are mathematical models. To build and develop such models requires a working knowledge of geometry and trigonometry.

The CCEA specification requires that students should be able to:
- calculate areas of triangles, circumferences and areas of circles, surface areas and volumes of rectangular blocks, cylinders and spheres
- use Pythagoras' theorem and the angle sum of a triangle
- use sin, cos and tan in physical problems
- understand the relationship between degrees and radians and translate from one to the other

Calculating areas, circumferences, surface areas and volumes

Table 5 shows some useful ideas you are likely to encounter in your course.

Table 5 Useful mathematical ideas

Practical activity	Shape	Equation
Area under a velocity–time graph for a body with constant acceleration (i) from rest, and (ii) from a non-zero starting velocity	(i) triangle (ii) trapezium	area = $\frac{1}{2}$(base × height) area = $\frac{1}{2}$(sum of parallels) × height
Calculating the distance travelled by a planet in a single (assumed circular) orbit	circle, radius r	circumference = $2\pi r = \pi d$
Calculating the cross-section area of a wire	circle, radius r	area = $\pi r^2 = \frac{\pi d^2}{4}$
Finding the density of the material of a ball bearing	sphere, radius r	volume = $(\frac{4}{3})\pi r^3$
Estimating the volume of gas in a typical room	cuboid, sides a, b, c	volume = $a \times b \times c$
Calculating the volume of gas in a cylinder	cylinder, radius r, height h	volume = $\pi r^2 h$
Calculating the energy arriving from the Sun per unit area of the Earth	sphere, radius r	Surface area = $4\pi r^2$

Mathematical content

Pythagoras' theorem and the trigonometrical functions

When adding and resolving vectors (such as forces), a knowledge of trigonometry is essential.

Pythagoras' theorem applies only to right-angled triangles (Figure 9). It states that, if the sides of a right-angled triangle are a, b and h (where h is the hypotenuse), then:

$$h^2 = a^2 + b^2$$

Right-angled triangles are also used to define the trigonometrical functions: sine, cosine and tangent.

$$\sin \theta = \frac{\text{opposite}}{\text{hypotenuse}} = \frac{O}{H} \qquad \cos \theta = \frac{\text{adjacent}}{\text{hypotenuse}} = \frac{A}{H}$$

$$\tan \theta = \frac{\text{opposite}}{\text{adjacent}} = \frac{O}{A}$$

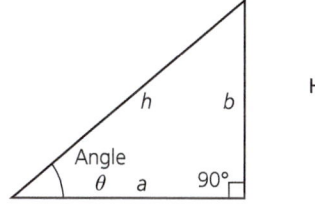 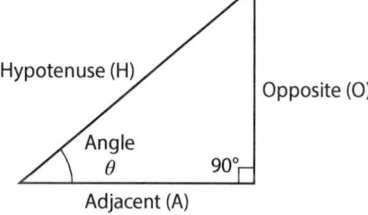

Figure 9 Pythagoras theorem and the trigonometrical functions

> **Knowledge check 13**
>
> A metal pipe of length 120 cm has an internal diameter of 12 mm and an external diameter of 15 mm. Calculate the volume of metal in the pipe.

> **Knowledge check 14**
>
> A proton is known to have a mass of 1.66×10^{-27} kg. The density of the matter in the proton is thought to be 2.3×10^{17} kg m^{-3}. Calculate the radius of the proton, assuming it to be a sphere.

> **Exam tip**
>
> If you have to find a volume in m^3 (or an area in m^2), convert lengths given in the question to metres before carrying out the calculation.

Worked example

A student working on a force board in a laboratory models three forces in equilibrium and draws the free body diagram shown in Figure 10. Calculate the sizes of the forces F and W.

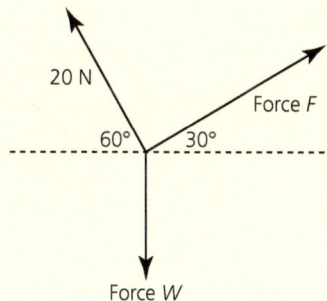

Figure 10 Forces in equilibrium

Answer

From Figure 11(a) we see that the horizontal component of the 20 N force is $20 \cos 60°$.

From Figure 11(b) we see that the horizontal component of force F is $F \cos 30°$.

Since W has no horizontal component, then $20 \cos 60° = F \cos 30°$.

Dividing both sides by $\cos 30°$ gives $F = (20 \cos 60°)/\cos 30° = 11.55$ N.

From Figure 11(a) we see that the vertical component of the 20 N force is $20 \sin 60°$.

> **Exam tip**
>
> The mnemonic SOHCAHTOA (pronounced socatoa) is a useful way to remember what is meant by sin, cos and tan.

Content Guidance

From Figure 11(b) we see that the vertical component of force F is $F \sin 30°$ = 11.55 sin 30°.

Since these two vertical components are in equilibrium with W, then $W = 20 \sin 60° + 11.55 \sin 30° = 23.10$ N.

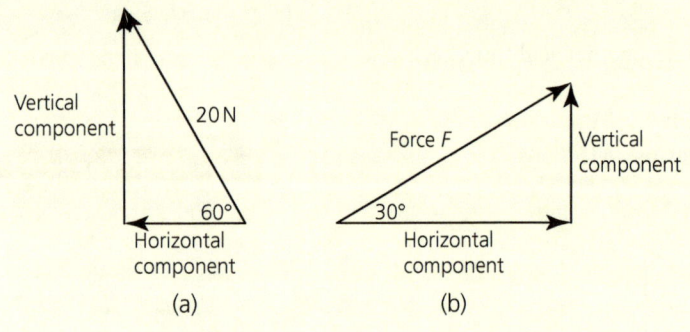

Figure 11 Triangles of forces

The relationship between degrees and radians

In most situations, angles are measured in degrees. Sometimes, such as in the study of motion in a circle or simple harmonic motion, this is inappropriate. Then it is much better to work in radians.

A radian is defined as the angle subtended by the arc of a circle equal in length to the radius and is approximately equal to 57.3°. The exact conversion is 180° = π radians. This is why angles in radians are frequently written in terms of π.

Angle θ is equal to 1 radian if the arc length s is equal to the circle's radius (Figure 12).

Why are radians so useful? The answer is that they greatly simplify circular measures, as shown in Table 6.

Table 6 Degree and radian formulae

	Formula (θ is in degrees)	Formula (θ is in radians)
Length of arc s	$s = \left(\dfrac{\theta}{360}\right) \times 2\pi r$	$s = r\theta$
Area of sector A	$A = \left(\dfrac{\theta}{360}\right) \times \pi r^2$	$A = \frac{1}{2} r^2 \theta$

> **Exam tip**
> When calculating arc length or sector areas, it does not matter if your calculator is set to radians or degrees. However, it must be set to radians if you are finding trigonometrical ratios and the angles are in radians.

> **Knowledge check 15**
> Set your calculator to radians and find (in radians) the angles θ if (a) $\sin \theta = 0.5$, (b) $\cos \theta = 0.5$, (c) $\tan \theta = 1$, (d) $\cos \theta = 1$. Then repeat to find the values of θ in degrees.

> **Knowledge check 16**
> Convert the following angles to radians: (a) 30°, (b) 50°, (c) 60°, (d) 80°.

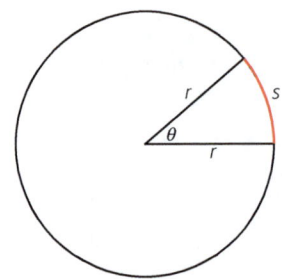

Figure 12 Definition of the radian

> **Knowledge check 17**
> What is the sum, in radians, of the three angles in a triangle?

Practical skills

Both the AS 3 and the A2 3 units have two components. AS 3A and A2 3A assess your ability to carry out experimental procedures in a laboratory. During your course you may have carried out practical work in a small group, but in the practical examinations you are working on your own.

While the emphasis is on assessing the transferable, practical skills you have encountered during your course, you may be asked to demonstrate your analytical skills and your ability to evaluate the reliability of data and the conclusions which might be drawn from it. You will also be required to demonstrate your mathematical skills and your ability to refine and develop experimental techniques. Since this is a written assessment, you are expected to be able to communicate observations, measurements, results and conclusions in an appropriate and effective manner.

In AS 3A, you are required to do four short experiments, spending 15 minutes on each. In A2 3A, you will carry out two experiments, spending 30 minutes on each.

There are no specific experiments that you must learn for these practical assessments. It is certainly expected that during your course you will have done all the experiments set down in the specification. However, many of these experiments require a much longer time than is available in the AS 3 and A2 3 assessments. In addition, many of the experiments carried out during your course must be done in small groups because there is insufficient apparatus to enable every student to do the work individually. This is why the emphasis is on the assessment of your practical *skills*. Each of the experiments from the specification is covered in the Practical activities section of this guide to help you to think through and apply your learning from carrying out each of them in preparation for the assessment.

AS 3B and A2 3B seek to assess your practical knowledge and your skills of data analysis, each in a 1 hour written exam paper. Considerable attention will be paid to the techniques of data analysis later in this book.

Altogether AS 3 is worth 20% of all the marks for the AS qualification and A2 3 accounts for 12% of the A-level qualification.

Physics is a practical subject, and experimental work should form a significant part of your AS or A-level physics course. It is commonly acknowledged that it is easier to learn and remember things if you have actually done them rather than having read about them or been told about them. That is why this section of the book is illustrated throughout by experiments, usually with a set of data for you to work through and questions to answer.

As you complete practical work during your physics course, you will develop skills in the use of a range of apparatus and techniques. Examination questions will test your knowledge and understanding of these techniques.

This section of the practical guide is in five main parts, which reflect an orderly approach to practical work and the approach taken in the subject specification:
- implementing
- analysis
- evaluation
- refinement
- communication

Content Guidance

Implementing

You are unlikely to be asked to produce a detailed plan in AS 3, but you may be asked to do so in A2 3. This is simply because you are limited to 15 minutes per experiment in AS 3, but you have 30 minutes per experiment in A2 3.

What is meant by implementing? The CCEA specification makes it clear that you must be able to:

- assemble and use measuring apparatus correctly, skilfully and effectively with full regard for safety, including:
  - spring and top-pan balances (mass)
  - ruler, micrometer and callipers (length)
  - graduated cylinder (liquid volume)
  - clock and stopwatch (time)
  - thermometer and sensor (temperature)
  - ammeter (electric current)
  - voltmeter (potential difference)
  - multimeter (resistance, p.d., current)
  - protractor (angle)
- use and describe how the cathode ray oscilloscope (CRO) can be used to determine the voltage and frequency (**A2 only**)
- make and record sufficient relevant, reliable and valid observations and measurements to the appropriate degree of precision and accuracy, using data loggers where suitable
- show familiarity with both analogue and digital displays

In AS 3A and A2 3A, you are unlikely to be asked which apparatus you should select to do a particular task. However, most certainly you will be required to assemble and use it.

An outline plan

Once the problem has been identified, you may be asked to produce an outline plan. Time constraints in AS 3A and A2 3A mean that a *detailed* description of what you plan to do is seldom required.

In almost all practical activities, the required apparatus is set out for you, often unassembled. The issue will not be what apparatus to use, but *how* to use it and *what* measurements must be made.

Examples of the use of apparatus listed in the specification (see Table 7) will be covered in the Practical activities chapter of this book. It cannot be emphasised enough that the skills to use apparatus effectively can be learnt— but learning skills takes time and practice in experimental activity.

You will also need to be able to consider strategies and techniques to ensure accurate results. For example, in nearly every AS 3A practical there is an experiment involving a stopwatch. If you are measuring the period of a pendulum you need to know how many oscillations to time. You also need to have learned, through practice, the relevant technique. For example, only a poor experimentalist will start the stopwatch at the same time as the bob is released. The examiner will not see you apply these techniques, but they will be critical if you are to obtain satisfactory results.

Practical skills

Table 7 Apparatus used in the practical activities

Apparatus	Practical activities
Spring and top-pan balances (mass)	1, 2, 5, 6, 15, 20, 21
Ruler, micrometer and callipers (length)	1, 3, 4, 5, 6, 12, 13, 14, 15, 16, 17, 18, 19, 21
Graduated cylinder (liquid volume)	1
Clock and stopwatch (time)	3, 20, 21, 22
Thermometer and sensor (temperature)	10
Ammeter (electric current)	7, 8, 9, 11, 20, 22
Voltmeter (potential difference)	7, 8, 9, 11, 20, 22
Multimeter (resistance, p.d., current)	7, 8, 9, 10, 11
Protractor (angle)	12, 13
Cathode ray oscilloscope (voltage and frequency)	23

Where relevant, safety issues will also be examined. Vague statements are unacceptable at this level. Your discussion must be relevant and well argued. You may also be asked what action the experimenter might take to minimise these risks. For example, in some electrical experiments the apparatus might get hot, causing a possible risk of burns to the skin. To reduce the risk, the apparatus might be set on a heat-proof mat and the electrical supply is switched on only when necessary.

Variables

You will be expected to identify the types of variables in *any* experiment you are asked to plan and carry out. You therefore need to be able to identify the **independent**, **dependent** and **control** variables in every experiment you do.

Independent variable
The variable for which values are changed by the experimenter.

Dependent variable
The variable for which the value is measured in the experiment.

Control variables
Variables other than the independent variable, which could affect the outcome of the investigation and therefore have to be kept constant.

> **Worked example**
>
> A student investigates how the frequency of a simple pendulum varies when the length of the string increases. What are the independent, dependent and control variables in this experiment?
>
> **Answer**
>
> The independent variable is the length of the string.
>
> The dependent variable is the period of the pendulum's oscillation. It is from this that the frequency is calculated.
>
> The control variable is the mass of the pendulum bob.

Accuracy and precision

The accuracy of any experiment you do depends on two factors: the equipment used and your technique. It is important that you can distinguish between accuracy and precision.

The more accurate you are in making a measurement, the closer you are to the true value.

One way to improve **accuracy** is to repeat and then average. For example, suppose five students measure the length of the same metal wire with a metre ruler with a centimetre scale and get the following results: 91 cm, 93 cm, 90 cm, 92 cm, 89 cm. The mean of these results is 91 cm and that is probably the most accurate length possible from these data. Another way to improve accuracy is to use a better

Accuracy Accuracy is how close we get to the true value of any physical measurement.

Practical techniques and data analysis 25

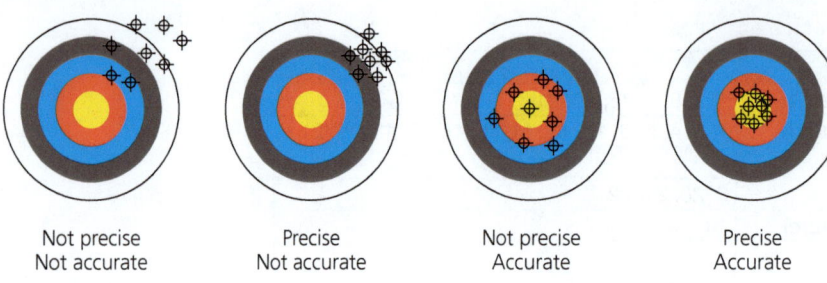

Not precise / Not accurate   Precise / Not accurate   Not precise / Accurate   Precise / Accurate

Figure 13 Accuracy and precision

measuring instrument. A digital voltmeter, for example, is likely to be more accurate than an analogue meter.

Precise measurements are those where the range is small. For example, suppose three students measure the mass of a beaker using balance A. They get the results 45.7 g, 45.9 g and 45.8 g. The range of these measurements is 45.9 − 45.7 = 0.2 g. That is the extent of their **precision**.

But you need to be careful. A stopwatch with a sweeping hand might have a **resolution** of 0.1 s while a digital stopwatch might have a resolution of 0.01 s. However, both stopwatches have a similar precision because this factor will be determined by the reaction time of the person using it.

Precision Precision measures the extent to which measurements are the same.

Resolution Resolution is the fineness to which an instrument can be read.

Dataloggers

It is no exaggeration to say that dataloggers have revolutionised the work of the professional physicist. They enable the easy collection and analysis of huge volumes of data over long periods of time with limited involvement of staff. For the A-level physicist, they are increasingly being used in schools and colleges and this is recognised in the CCEA specification.

Where you have experience of using them, use your knowledge in written papers. However, you are unlikely to be asked to use a datalogger in units AS 3A and A2 3A because some schools will not have them and they represent a substantial financial cost.

While you can use a datalogger in most experiments, they are specifically used in Practical activities 4, 5, 6, 8, 25 and 26. Remember that there are always alternatives to the use of dataloggers which will be acceptable to the GCE examiners.

Analysis

The specification states what you are expected to be able to do by way of analysis. Briefly, the expectation is that you can:

- present work appropriately in written, tabular, graphical or other forms
- analyse, interpret and explain your own and others' experimental and investigative activities, using ICT and other methods
- show awareness of the limitations of experimental measurements when commenting on trends and patterns in the data
- draw valid conclusions by applying knowledge and understanding of physics

Practical skills

Making and recording observations

You need to know how to record the results of an investigation. In almost all practical work in physics, you record results in a table.

When drawing tables and recording data ensure that:
- The lines in your table are drawn with a ruler and pencil.
- There are headings for each column and/or row.
- There are units for each column and/or row – always placed after a solidus with the heading, for example, 'speed/cm s^{-1}'.
- Units are not written beside the numbers in the table.
- There is enough space for repeat measurements and averages. Remember, the more repeats you do, the more reliable the data.
- Data items are recorded to the same number of decimal places or significant figures.

Be aware that *only* the solidus notation is acceptable by CCEA's A-level examiners when entering headings in a table or labelling the axes on a graph. So, an acceptable label is speed/cm s^{-1}.

But the solidus notation is *never* acceptable when expressing *units*. For units, only the index notation is acceptable. So, for the unit of specific heat capacity, the unit $J\,kg^{-1}\,K^{-1}$ is acceptable, but J/kg K is unacceptable.

When showing the labels and units on the axes of graphs, the same rules apply. The quantity and units shown on the axes should be *identical* to those in the table.

In A2 3 (but not AS 3), you might be required to use natural logarithms. Logarithms themselves have no units, so, for example, a logarithmic entry in a table for a current I in amperes might be headed ln (I/A). The common error is to write ln I/A. This implies that ln I has units of amperes, when in fact, only I has units of amperes, ln I is dimensionless.

The same is true of the exponential function e. For example, in an experiment on capacitor discharge, the voltage decreases exponentially, that is:

$$V = V_0 \times e^{-t/RC}$$

Although V, t, R and C all have units, the quantity $e^{-t/RC}$ is dimensionless – it has no units.

The limitations of experimental measurements
Errors

To a physicist, an error is not a mistake. It is the difference between a measured result and the true value or accepted value and can be due to random or systematic effects.

Random errors

If you ask a group of students to measure the height of their teacher, it is almost certain that there will be a range of results obtained. Some will be too high and some will be too low. This kind of error is called a random error. Random errors cannot be eliminated, but their effect can be mitigated. This is done by repeating and averaging and by plotting a graph. By doing so, the results that are too high will cancel out with those that are too low.

> **Exam tip**
> It is particularly useful to show how results might be set out in a table with suitable headings and units when planning a practical or quickly demonstrating in an exam what measurements have to be taken.

> **Knowledge check 18**
> What type of error is represented by the graph in Figure 14?

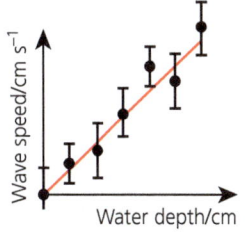

Figure 14 Error bars

There are always random errors present when we use any instrument. We can identify random errors when we see that some results are a little higher than we might expect and some are a little lower. If we plot a graph of the data, we will observe some points slightly above the line of best fit and some points slightly below it.

Systematic errors

A systematic error produces measurements that are consistently too large or too small, usually by the same amount. This could be caused by recording the wrong unit, poor technique (e.g. reading from a scale at an angle, causing parallax error), failure to check for zero error, or incorrect calibration of the instrument.

> **Knowledge check 19**
>
> Figure 15 shows a Vernier scale as might be seen on callipers when the jaws are fully closed.
>
>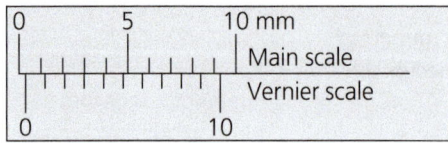
>
> **Figure 15** Vernier scale
>
> a What is the size of the zero error shown?
>
> b When used to measure the diameter of a coin, the scale reading is 7.5 mm. What is the coin's actual diameter?

Exam tip

If you come across an instrument with a zero error in a practical examination, raise your hand and tell the supervisor. If it was unintentional, the supervisor will put it right. If it was intentional, adjust your readings accordingly.

Uncertainty in measurements

There is an uncertainty in every measurement due to the instrument being used. When we say the length of a pencil is 195 mm long, we mean that it is not 194 or 196 mm, it is 195 mm. But what does that mean exactly? It means that the pencil's length lies between 194.5 mm and 195.5 mm. If it were just less than 194.5 mm, we would have said the length was 194 mm; if it were just more than 195.5 mm, we would have said its length was 196 mm. If we take a single reading on a mm scale the uncertainty is therefore ±0.5 mm.

Generally, the **uncertainty** in a *single reading* is ± (half of the smallest scale division of the instrument). However, when we use an instrument, such as a ruler, we implicitly take two readings – the start reading (usually at zero) and the final reading. Our measurement then is the difference between these readings. So, the uncertainties in each reading combine. In the case of the pencil, we might be subtracting 0 ± 0.5 mm from 195 ± 0.5 mm. This gives 195 ± 1 mm. We say the absolute uncertainty in the measurement is ±1 mm.

Similarly, when we add (or subtract) two measurements, we add the absolute uncertainty in each.

Uncertainty The uncertainty in a measurement is ±1 of the smallest scale division on the instrument.

Other factors affecting the uncertainty in a measurement

Sometimes the resolution of the instrument is not the limiting factor. An A-level physicist needs to be aware of this and be conscious of the cause of error in all measurements. The following examples should help you understand how the uncertainties involved are actually much larger than those due to the resolution of the measuring instrument.

Practical skills

In some experiments, you will be timing events with a stopwatch. A digital stopwatch typically has a resolution of 0.01 s, but the reaction time of the person using it is likely to be around 0.2 s or more. You should record the full reading on the stopwatch (e.g. 28.92 s) and reduce this to a more appropriate number of significant figures at a later stage, e.g. after averaging readings. To reduce the percentage uncertainty in your measurement, it is also helpful to design the experiment in such a way that the times being measured are 30 seconds or more. This is one of the reasons why you should measure the time for about 20 oscillations (rather than just one) when determining the period of a simple pendulum.

If you are finding the focal length of a lens, you may have to use a ruler to measure the distance from the centre of the lens to a sharp image on a screen. The ruler will probably be calibrated in mm and you may think your measurement is correct to within ±1 mm. But think again! The instruction is to obtain a sharp image. And there is almost certainly a range of distances over which the image is equally sharp. Typically, this range is around 4 mm. So the limiting instrument here is the human eye, which leads to an uncertainty closer to ±4 mm.

The uncertainty of the reading from digital meters (such as voltmeters and frequency meters) depends on the tolerance quoted by the manufacturer, and you may not always be told this. If you do not know it, you should always state uncertainty to ±1 of the last digit on the display.

Absolute and relative uncertainty

When we combine measurements, percentage uncertainty is much more useful. But first we need to know the absolute uncertainty in each measurement.

> **Knowledge check 20**
>
> a What does the Vernier scale shown in Figure 16 read? The numbers on the upper scale are in cm.
>
>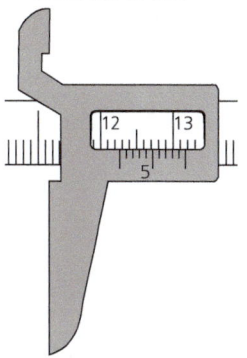
>
> **Figure 16** Callipers
>
> b What is the absolute uncertainty in the measurement?

Worked example

A student measures the mass of a liquid and finds it to be 93 ± 1 g. She then measures the volume of the liquid and finds it to be 62 ± 3 cm³. Calculate:

a the percentage uncertainty in the mass and the volume of the liquid
b the best value for the density of the liquid
c the percentage uncertainty in the density
d the absolute uncertainty in the density
e State the density of this liquid as it might be recorded in a practical experiment together with its associated absolute uncertainty.

Answer

a percentage uncertainty = $\dfrac{\text{absolute uncertainty}}{\text{best value of measurement}} \times 100\%$

The percentage uncertainty in the mass of the liquid is: $\dfrac{1}{93} \times 100\% = 1.1\%$.

The percentage uncertainty in the volume of the liquid is: $\dfrac{3}{62} \times 100\% = 4.8\%$.

b density = $\dfrac{\text{mass}}{\text{volume}} = \dfrac{93}{62} = 1.5 \, \text{g cm}^{-3}$

c The percentage uncertainty in a combined measurement obtained by multiplying or dividing two quantities is simply the sum of the percentage uncertainties.

> **Exam tip**
>
> Sometimes you are asked to state the absolute uncertainty in a measurement. Always quote the uncertainty to the same number of decimal places as the measurement itself. So, if the measurement is 12.8 cm, the uncertainty will be ± 0.1 cm.

Practical techniques and data analysis

Content Guidance

$$\begin{aligned}\text{percentage uncertainty in the density} &= \text{percentage uncertainty in the mass} + \text{percentage uncertainty in the volume}\\ &= 1.1\% + 4.8\%\\ &= 5.9\%\end{aligned}$$

d The absolute uncertainty in the density is therefore 5.9% of $1.5\,\text{g cm}^{-3} = 0.09\,\text{g cm}^{-3}$.

e density of liquid $= 1.5 \pm 0.09\,\text{g cm}^{-3}$

Powers

Often the mathematical calculations in physics involve the use of powers. For example, the volume V of a sphere is given by the formula:

$$V = \frac{4}{3}\pi r^3$$

What is the percentage uncertainty in the volume if the uncertainty in the radius r is ±1.5%?

Note that r^3 is simply a repeated product: $r^3 = r \times r \times r$. So, using the ideas of certainty in products, the uncertainty in V is simply $3 \times$ the uncertainty in r.

The percentage uncertainty in V is therefore $3 \times 1.5\% = 4.5\%$.

Combined uncertainties

In experiments, measurements are often made using several instruments and then used to calculate a quantity. The combined uncertainty can be found as follows.
- If quantities are added or subtracted, add the absolute uncertainties of each quantity.
- If quantities are multiplied or divided, add the percentage uncertainties of each quantity.
- If a quantity is raised to a power, then multiply the percentage uncertainty by the power.

Analysis and interpretation of experimental data

Much of the analysis carried out by A-level physics students involves mapping a non-linear equation to a linear form, plotting a straight-line graph and then interpreting it. This was dealt with in the Mathematical content section.

Evaluation

Carrying out experiments accurately and analysing the data obtained are only part of the expectations of you as an A-level physicist. You are expected to be able to reflect on the experiment critically. This means there is an expectation that you can:
- assess the reliability of data, results and conclusions drawn from the data
- evaluate the methodology used in and the impact of the experimental activity, and demonstrate an appreciation of their limitations
- calculate the absolute and percentage uncertainty in a quantity

Experimental data are reliable if they are reproduceable and valid. This is one of the reasons why professional physicists repeat the research carried out by others. For the A-level physicist, it is why repetition is so important. It ensures that inappropriate

---

Knowledge check 21

A physicist measures the thickness of a thin copper pipe using callipers. She does this by subtracting the internal diameter from the external diameter and dividing by 2. Why is the % error in the thickness likely to be unacceptably high?

conclusions are not drawn from insufficient data. Valid data mean the information gathered must be relevant. For example, in investigating the acceleration of a trolley down a runway, the trolley's mass is relevant, but its colour is not. Only when reliable, valid data are analysed can appropriate conclusions be drawn.

The experimental physicist is also expected to reflect on the methodology used. Are there better ways to carry out the investigation? There are limits to the experience gained in an A-level course, but, nevertheless, you are expected to be conscious of where improvements in an experiment might be made and where improvements are likely to be of limited value. For example, in an experiment to measure the resistivity of the material from which a piece of wire is made, it is quite appropriate to use a metre stick to measure the length to the nearest mm, but totally inappropriate to measure the diameter of the wire to the same precision.

As part of evaluating, you need to ask yourself questions such as:
- Was the experimental method suitable?
- What were the limitations in the methodology?
- What were the main sources of error?
- How could the method be improved to reduce or eliminate known sources of error?

Refinement

Even after evaluating the planning, methodology, data collection and so on, the reflective physicist will always ask 'how could I have done the task better?' CCEA calls this process refinement. The expectation is that you are able to:
- suggest improved effective and safe procedures, after considering quantitative and qualitative methods
- modify procedures in response to serious sources of **systematic** and **random error** in order to generate results that are as accurate and **reliable** as the apparatus allows

Often these improvements will be very simple indeed.

Communication

You are probably aware that the World Wide Web, invented in 1989 by the British engineer and computer scientist Tim Berners-Lee, was an attempt to enable physicists throughout the world to communicate more effectively. Communication of ideas is at the heart of what physicists do. As an A-level physicist you are expected to be able to:
- communicate observations, measurements, results and conclusions in an appropriate and effective manner

While mathematics lies at the heart of physics, it is essential that you can communicate in the way that is most appropriate. In some cases, experimental results might best be communicated graphically. Conclusions to investigative work are normally required to be written in academic English, using the appropriate scientific vocabulary. While in everyday speech, no distinction is made between mass and weight, in the language of physics they are entirely different quantities and examiners expect you to understand that and use the words appropriately.

Random error One that causes a measurement to differ from the true value by different amounts each time, some positive and some negative.

Systematic error One that causes a measurement to differ from the true value by the same amount each time.

Reliability A test is defined as reliable if different scientists repeating the same experiment or measurement consistently get the same results.

Exam tip
It is important to learn the definitions of technical terms accurately if you are to use them effectively in written exams.

Content Guidance

Practical activities

Practical activity in this book	Practical in CCEA specification Appendix 4	Coverage in CCEA specification
1 Determine the density of a solid or liquid	1	
2 Determine (a) the value of an unknown mass and (b) the mass of a uniform ruler using the principle of moments	2, 3	
3 Determine the acceleration of free fall by means of a falling object and light gates	4	
4 Verification of the mathematical form of Newton's second law	5, 6	
5 Verification of the conservation of linear momentum in a collision	7	
6 Investigate the energy exchange between potential and kinetic for a falling body	8	
7 Determine resistance by the ammeter–voltmeter method and using a multimeter or ohmmeter and the I–V characteristics of a metallic conductor at constant temperature and a filament lamp	9, 12, 13	1.10.1 and 1.10.10
8 Verify the relationships for resistors in (a) series and (b) parallel	10	
9 Determine the resistivity of a material	11	1.10.6
10 Determine the resistance–temperature characteristic of a negative temperature coefficient (ntc) thermistor	14	1.10.13
11 Determine the e.m.f. and internal resistance of a battery	15	1.11.3
12 Verify Snell's law and determine the refractive index of a material	16, 17	2.2.1
13 Determine the critical angle of glass or Perspex® using a semicircular block	18	
14 Determine the focal length of a converging lens and verify experimentally the lens equation for real images	19	2.3.3
15 Verify that the magnification of a real image is equal to the ratio of the image distance to the object distance	20	
16 Determine the speed of sound in air using a resonance tube	21	2.4.6
17 Determine the wavelength of light using a double slit	22	
18 Determine the wavelength of light using a diffraction grating	22	
19 Determine the Young modulus for the material of a metal wire		4.1.5
20 Perform and demonstrate an electrical method for determining specific heat capacity (of a liquid)		4.2.8
21 Investigate experimentally the motion of the simple pendulum and the loaded spiral spring		4.4.3
22 Describe experiments to demonstrate the discharge and charge of a capacitor and measure the time constant		5.4.6 and 5.4.10
23 Describe how the cathode ray oscilloscope (CRO) can be used to determine the voltage and frequency		6.1.2

Practical activities

Practical activity 1

Determine the density of a solid or liquid

Background information and practical procedure

The density of a material is given by the equation:

$$\text{density} = \frac{\text{mass}}{\text{volume}}$$

Three situations are considered here – a regular solid, an irregular solid and a liquid.

1. **A regularly shaped object (such as a small solid metal cuboid)**

   The method involves finding the mass of the solid using a digital top-pan balance and its length, breadth and height using callipers.

   The volume of the cylinder is then calculated using the formula:

   $$\text{volume} = \text{length} \times \text{breadth} \times \text{height}$$

2. **An irregularly shaped object (such as a piece of concrete)**

   Again, the mass is found using a top-pan balance. The volume is found by the displacement method using a graduated cylinder, as in Figure 17.

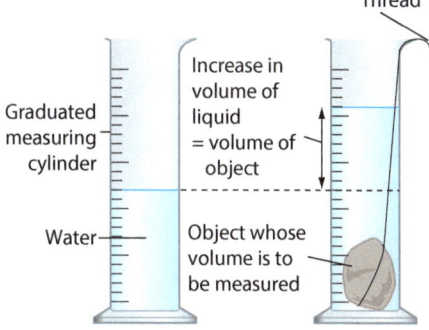

Figure 17 Finding the volume of a lump of concrete

3. **A liquid**

   The mass is found with a top-pan balance and a measuring cylinder. The volume is found from the graduations on the measuring cylinder, as in Figure 18.

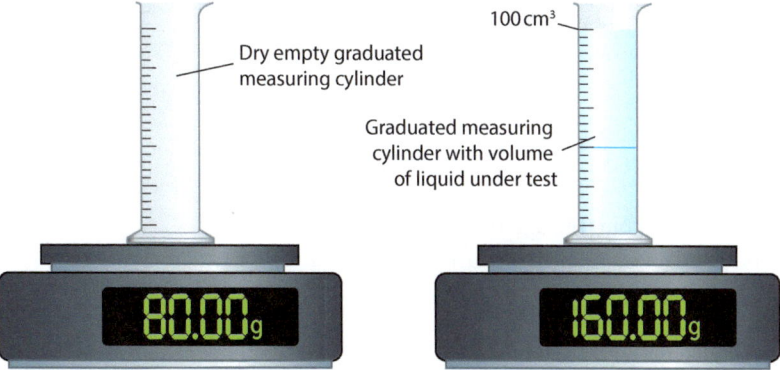

Figure 18 Finding the mass of a known volume of liquid

Practical techniques and data analysis 33

Content Guidance

Safety

Density experiments frequently use glassware. It is important that every precaution is taken to prevent beakers and measuring cylinders rolling off the bench and smashing into small, dangerous pieces. If this happens, the laboratory supervisor should be informed, the experiment suspended and steps taken to clean up the area in the vicinity of the accident.

Worked example 1

A regular solid

The mass of a regular solid in the form of a cuboid is found to be 75.62 ± 0.01 g. Its dimensions are measured using callipers and found to be:

length: 31.2 ± 0.1 mm   breadth: 24.5 ± 0.1 mm   height 15.5 ± 0.1 mm

a Calculate the density of the solid.
b Calculate the uncertainty in the density.

Answer

a density = $\dfrac{\text{mass}}{\text{volume}} = \dfrac{75.62}{3.12 \times 2.45 \times 1.55} = 6.38 \, \text{g cm}^{-3}$

b % uncertainty in length = $\dfrac{0.1}{31.2} \times 100\% = \pm 0.32\%$

% uncertainty in breadth = $\dfrac{0.1}{24.5} \times 100\% = \pm 0.41\%$

% uncertainty in height = $\dfrac{0.1}{15.5} \times 100\% = \pm 0.65\%$

% uncertainty in volume = $0.32\% + 0.41\% + 0.65\% = \pm 1.38\%$

% uncertainty in mass = $\dfrac{0.01}{75.62} \times 100\% = \pm 0.01\%$

% uncertainty in density = % uncertainty in mass + % uncertainty in volume = $\pm 1.39\%$

Worked example 2

A liquid

Various volumes of liquid are poured into a measuring cylinder and, in each case, the total mass of the measuring cylinder and its contents are recorded, as in Table 8.

Table 8 Experimental data

Mass of liquid + container/g	76.0	92.0	108.0	124.0	140.0
Volume of liquid/cm^3	20.0	40.0	60.0	80.0	100.0

Plot the graph of mass of measuring cylinder and contents against volume and use the graph to find the density of the liquid and the mass of the measuring cylinder.

Answer

Mass of liquid plus container = (density of liquid × volume of liquid) + mass of container

or

$M = d \times V + m$

Practical activities

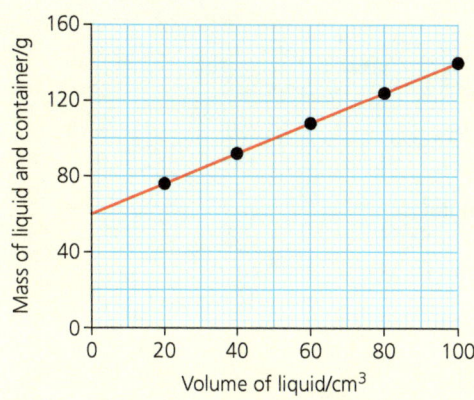

Figure 19 Graph to find the mass of a cylinder and liquid density

Map this equation against that of a straight line:

$$y = mx + c$$

M is equivalent to y, d is equivalent to gradient m, V is equivalent to x and m is equivalent to intercept c.

Gradient of graph = density $d = \dfrac{140 - 60}{100 - 0} = 0.8\,\text{g cm}^{-3}$

Mass of measuring cylinder m = intercept on vertical axis = 60 g

Practical activity 2

Determine (a) the value of an unknown mass and (b) the mass of a uniform ruler using the principle of moments

Background information

Here are three important definitions exemplified in this practical activity:

1. The centre of gravity (CoG) of an object is the point through which the entire weight of that object can be thought to act.
2. The moment of a force about a point is equal to the product of the force and the perpendicular distance from the point to the line-of-action of the force.
3. The principle of moments (PoM) states that for an object in equilibrium, the sum of the clockwise moments about any point is equal to the sum of the anticlockwise moments about the same point.

If a metre stick is suspended at its CoG, it may come to rest as a horizontal lever. An object of known mass at one side of the CoG may be balanced with another of unknown mass on the other. Applying the PoM then allows us to calculate the unknown force and hence the unknown weight.

If the metre stick is suspended at some point other than its CoM, then its own weight will cause it to tilt because of the unbalanced moment. If now we attach a known weight to restore equilibrium, we can use the PoM to determine the weight and hence the mass of the metre ruler itself.

Practical techniques and data analysis 35

Content Guidance

Practical procedure: finding an unknown mass

The essential parts of this experiment are:
1. Suspend and balance a metre ruler at the 50 cm mark using twine.
2. Hang a known mass m_1 on the left-hand side and the unknown mass m_u on the right-hand side of the 50 cm mark.
3. Adjust the position of these masses until the metre ruler is horizontal once again, as shown in Figure 20.
4. If we apply the PoM about the pivot, we see that: $m_1 g \times d_1 = m_u g \times d_2$.
5. Hence $m_u = \dfrac{m_1 \times d_1}{d_2}$
6. Repeat the experiment using different known masses, recording the results in a suitably headed table, and calculate an average value of m_u.

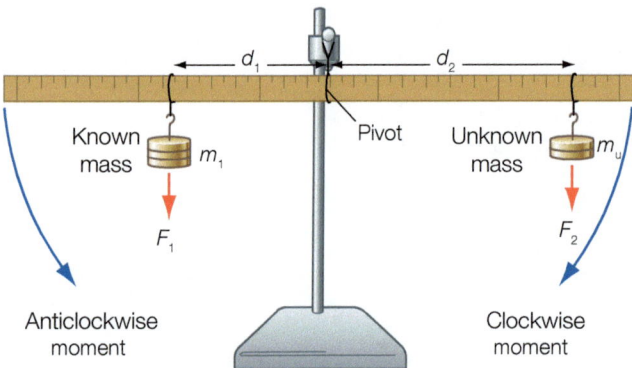

Figure 20 Finding an unknown mass

Practical procedure: finding the mass of a uniform metre ruler

> **Worked example**
>
> A pair of students work together to find the mass of a uniform metre ruler using the method above. The assembled apparatus is shown in Figure 21.
>
>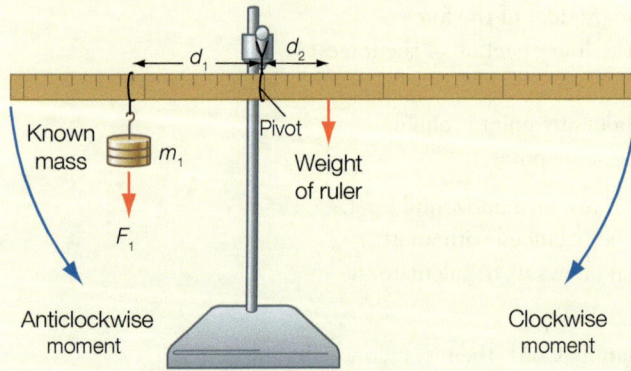
>
> **Figure 21** Finding the mass of a metre ruler

Practical activities

a Describe briefly the experimental procedure.
b Explain why, in this experiment, the ruler must not be balanced at its centre of mass.

The other student decides to plot a straight-line graph of their results in order to determine the mass of the metre ruler.

c Use the data below to plot a straight-line graph and use it to find the mass of the ruler.
The right-hand column is for your use.

m_1/g	d_1/cm	d_2/cm	
100	30.6	20.4	
200	15.3	20.4	
300	10.1	20.4	
400	7.7	20.4	
500	6.1	20.4	

Answer

a – Suspend and balance a metre ruler at around the 40 cm mark using twine.
 – Hang a known mass m_1 on the left-hand side of the ruler.
 – Adjust the position of this mass until the metre ruler is horizontal once again.
 – If we apply the PoM about the pivot, we see that: $m_1 g \times d_1 = m_R g \times d_2$, where m_R is the unknown mass of the ruler and d_2 is the distance from the pivot to the 50 cm mark.
 – Hence, $m_R = \dfrac{m_1 \times d_1}{d_2}$
 – Repeat the experiment using different known masses, and different values of d_1.
 – Record the results in a suitably headed table and calculate an average value of m_R.

b If the metre ruler was balanced at its CoM, the weight of the ruler would not have a moment about the point of suspension.

c

m_1/g	d_1/cm	d_2/cm	d_2/d_1
100	30.6	20.4	0.67
200	15.3	20.4	1.33
300	10.1	20.4	2.02
400	7.7	20.4	2.65
500	6.1	20.4	3.34

Rearranging the equation $m_1 g \times d_1 = m_R g \times d_2$ gives:

$$m_1 = m_R \times \dfrac{d_2}{d_1}$$

A graph of m_1 against the dimensionless ratio $\dfrac{d_2}{d_1}$ will therefore give a straight line through the origin with gradient equal to the mass of the ruler m_R.

Content Guidance

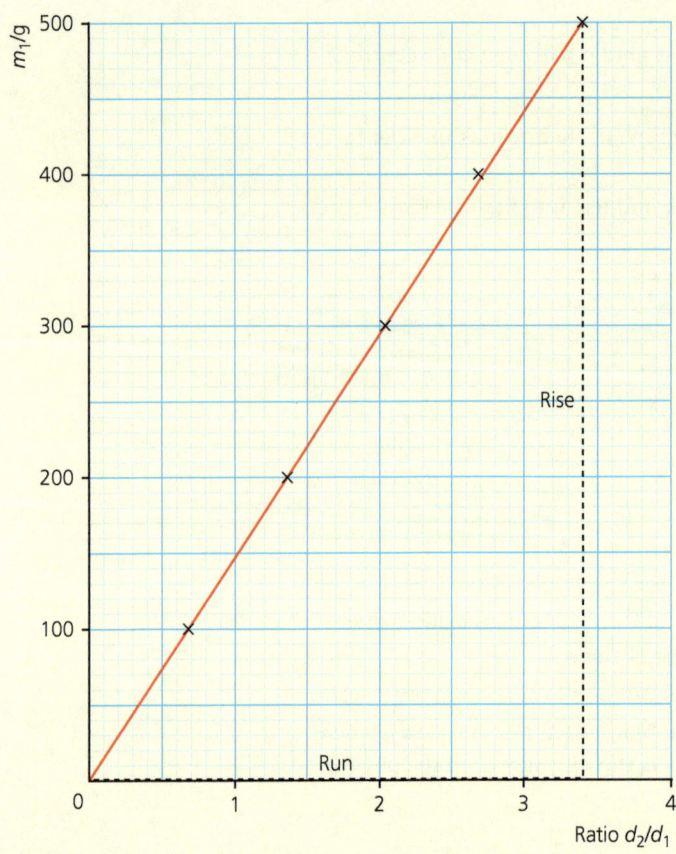

Figure 22 Finding the mass of a ruler graphically

Therefore, gradient = $\dfrac{\text{rise}}{\text{run}} = \dfrac{500}{3.4} = 147\,\text{g}$ = mass of ruler.

> **Knowledge check 22**
>
> The PoM is expressed in terms of moments of forces. Explain why both experiments do not need to use the value of g.

> **Exam tip**
>
> Remember, there are three aspects to the principle of moments: ACWM = CWM, about any point, when in equilibrium. The principle does not just relate to moments about the pivot.

Practical activity 3

Determine the acceleration of free fall by means of a falling object and light gates

Background information

A free-falling object means one that is falling vertically under gravity, with no other forces acting. All objects falling in air will experience *some* air resistance. But provided the object is made of a dense material and its speed is not too large, it may be considered to be falling freely. For such an object we can apply Newton's equation of uniformly accelerated motion:

$$v = u + gt$$

where u is the initial velocity, v is the final velocity, t is the elapsed time and g is the acceleration of free fall.

We map this to the general equation of a straight line through the origin: $y = c + mx$.

So, we would predict that a graph of v (vertical axis) against t (horizontal axis) would be a straight line of positive intercept u on the vertical axis, and with gradient g.

Practical procedure

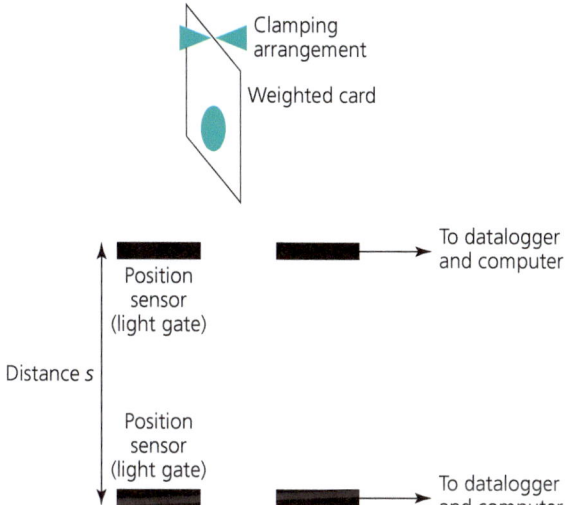

Figure 23 Free fall apparatus

Figure 23 shows one possible method. The important points are:

1. The weighted card is clamped a few cm above the upper light gate.
2. When released, the card must fall vertically between the light gates.
3. The datalogger requires the length of the card to be input in order to calculate its velocity v as it exits the lower light gate.
4. The time of fall t is changed by changing the position of the lower light gate, thus changing the distance s.
5. The datalogging software is set to print on-screen the values of v and t.
6. The values of v and t should be found at least three times and averaged for each distance s over as wide a range as possible.

Safety

The following precautions should be observed:

- Although a mains-operated laboratory power supply may be used to provide low voltages with the datalogger, care should be taken to prevent short circuits.
- A suitable container should be placed under the lower light gate to catch the falling card and prevent it creating a trip hazard.

Content Guidance

Worked example

Table 9 shows a set of results. For simplicity, the velocities and times indicated represent the average of three values for each distance. In practice, all values would be shown.

Table 9 Velocity and time data for a falling card

Time t/ms	Velocity v/m s^{-1}
150	1.40
200	1.91
250	2.40
300	2.69
350	3.10
400	3.50

a Plot the graph of v against t.
b Determine a value of g from your graph.
c State what the positive intercept on the vertical axis indicates and how, if the experiment were to be repeated, it might be reduced.
d Why might you want to repeat this experiment with different apparatus?

Answer

a The graph should be similar to that shown in Figure 24.

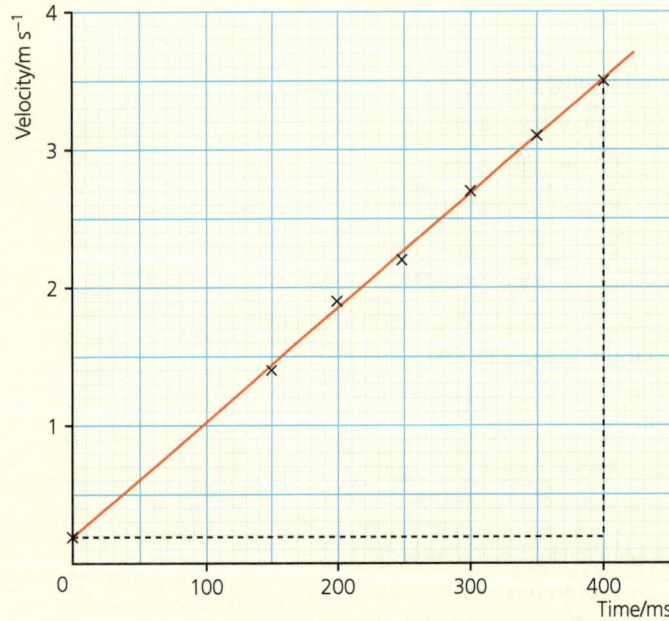

Figure 24 Velocity–time graph for a falling card

b The value of g = gradient = $\dfrac{3.50 - 0.20}{0.400 - 0} = \dfrac{3.30}{0.400} = 8.3 \text{ m s}^{-2}$.

c The intercept represents the velocity of the card as it entered the upper light gate. It might be reduced by keeping the distance between the bottom of the card and the upper light gate as small as possible.

d The data points are all close to the line of best fit, but the calculated value of g is significantly different from the accepted value, suggesting there is a systematic error in the measurement of velocity or time.

Exam tip

When finding a gradient from a graph, draw the largest possible triangle. This is good practice and is mentioned in the CCEA Mark Schemes and commented upon by the Chief Examiner in her report on the examination. It is important because it leads to minimal error in the calculated value of the gradient.

Practical activities

Knowledge check 23

A student uses the apparatus shown in Figure 25 to measure the times t taken for a metal ball bearing to fall from an electromagnet through measured distances h.

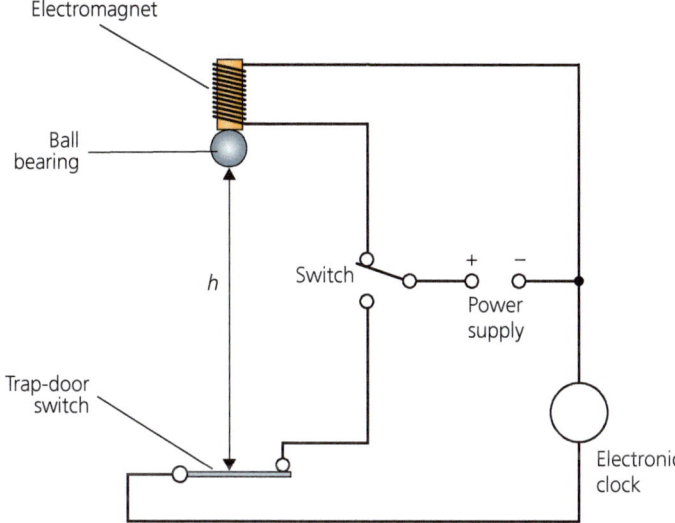

Figure 25 Finding g using an electromagnet

a What straight-line graph would the student plot to find the value of the acceleration of free fall g?

b How would the student find g from his graph?

Practical activity 4

Verification of the mathematical form of Newton's second law

a Acceleration is directly proportional to force for a constant mass.

b Acceleration is **inversely proportional** to mass for a constant force.

Background information

These experiments are important for two reasons:

1 They verify one form of Newton's second law ($F = ma$).
2 They lead to the definition of the newton as the force that gives a mass of 1 kg an acceleration of $1\,\mathrm{m\,s^{-2}}$.

At GCSE you will have encountered the mathematical form of Newton's second law. This can be rearranged as:

$$a = \frac{F}{m}$$

which can be interpreted as shown in the title to this practical activity.

However, the unit of force, the newton, can strictly only be defined once the results of these experiments have been established. We shall therefore, for the moment, *assume* that a mass of 100 g produces a gravitational force of 0.98 N.

Inversely proportional
Quantities are inversely proportional to each other if their product is constant.

Content Guidance

Practical procedure

The apparatus (Figure 26) required for both experiments is:
- wooden (or plastic) runway
- trolley
- double interrupt mask
- light gate and data logger
- slotted masses to be mounted on a hanger
- string
- top-pan balance (experiment 2 only)

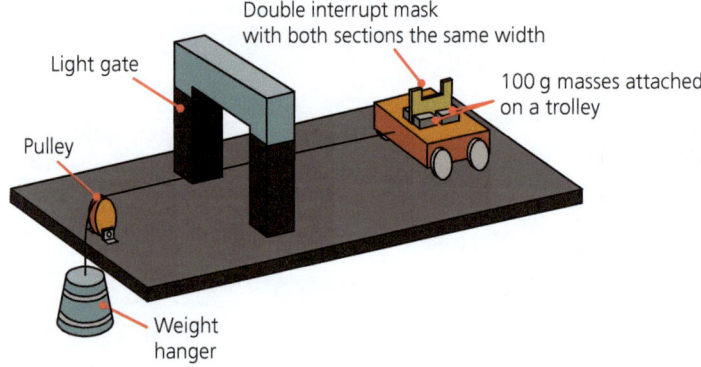

Figure 26 Apparatus for both experiments

Preparation for *both* experiments involves:

1. Compensate the runway for friction by tilting it until the trolley moves with a constant speed after it is given a gentle push.
2. Screw the clamped pulley to the runway so that it can hang over the edge of the bench.
3. Attach a length of string to the trolley and pass it over the clamped pulley to the mass hanger.
4. Position the light gate so that the trolley can pass through it without obstruction.
5. Ensure the mask on the trolley interrupts the light gate twice (double interrupt) before the masses hit the ground.
6. Enter via the datalogging software the lengths of the two interrupt masks (both the same) to enable the program to determine the acceleration.

Experiment 1 Acceleration is directly proportional to the applied force, for constant mass

1. Remove one of the 100 g masses on the trolley and attach it to the mass hanger.
2. Use the light gate to measure the acceleration of the trolley.
3. Carry out the procedure to find the acceleration several times until **repeatable**, reliable values are obtained.
4. Continue in this way, transferring 100 g masses at a time from the trolley until the acceleration is found for masses on the hanger ranging from 100 g to 600 g.

Repeatable Results are repeatable if similar results are obtained when an experiment is repeated by the same person several times.

Practical activities

Analysis of results

A careful experimentalist might obtain a set of results similar to those in Table 10.

Table 10 A typical set of results

Mass on hanger/g	100	200	300	400	500	600
Force/N	0.98	1.96	2.94	3.92	4.90	5.88
Acceleration/m s^{-2}	0.80	1.61	2.39	3.21	4.00	4.82
Acceleration/m s^{-2}	0.80	1.59	2.41	3.19	4.00	4.78
Mean acceleration/m s^{-2}	0.80	1.60	2.40	3.20	4.00	4.80

Worked example

a What graph should be plotted to illustrate the results of this experiment?
b Draw a sketch of the graph you would expect to obtain. You do not need to plot data points.
c What conclusion can be drawn from this graph?

Answer

a A graph of acceleration against force should be plotted.
b It should yield a straight line through the origin, as shown in Figure 27.

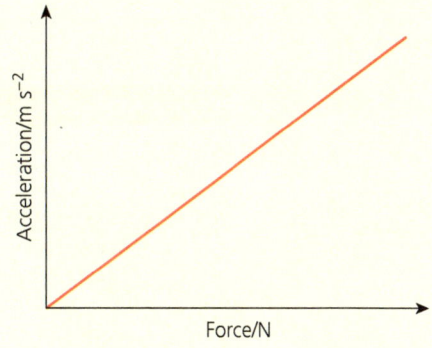

Figure 27 Graphical treatment of Newton's second law

c The graph confirms that acceleration is directly proportional to F, for a constant mass.

> **Knowledge check 24**
>
> Suggest why masses are transferred from the trolley in this experiment, rather than simply **adding** new masses to the hanger.

Experiment 2 Acceleration is inversely proportional to the mass, for a constant force

1 Choose a suitable value for the accelerating force F (e.g. around 4 N) provided by the falling weights. This remains constant throughout the experiment.
2 Weigh the trolley using a top-pan balance.
3 Use the light gate and datalogger to measure the acceleration of the trolley when accelerated by force F.
4 Carry out the procedure to find the acceleration several times until repeatable, reliable values are obtained.
5 Increase the mass being accelerated in steps of 1 kg up to about 6 kg, by attaching slotted masses to the trolley, and for each determine the acceleration using the light gate and datalogger.

Content Guidance

Analysis of results

A careful experimentalist might obtain a set of results similar to those in Table 11.

Table 11 A typical set of results

Mass being accelerated/kg	1.0	2.0	3.0	4.0	5.0	6.0
Acceleration/m s^{-2}	3.90	1.95	1.35	1.22	0.80	0.65
Acceleration/m s^{-2}	4.10	2.05	1.31	1.18	0.80	0.67
Mean acceleration/m s^{-2}	4.00	2.00	1.33	1.20	0.80	0.66

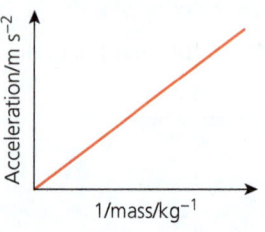

Figure 28 Demonstrating inverse proportion graphically

A graph of acceleration against the reciprocal of the mass should be plotted. It should yield a straight line through the origin confirming that acceleration is inversely proportional to the mass (Figure 28).

Worked example

a One of the results in Table 11 is an **outlier**, sometimes called a 'rogue result'. Which is it? Give a reason for your answer.
b What should an experimentalist do when such a result is obtained?
c How should the result be dealt with if a graph is to be plotted?

Answer

a The acceleration of the 4 kg mass is the outlier. For all of the other results, the product of the mean acceleration and the mass is constant (4 N). For the outlier, it is different (4.8 N).
b Repeat the experiment to find out whether the acceleration obtained for this mass was correct.
c Plot the point, but ignore it when drawing the line of best fit.

Outlier A value that lies outside the other values in a set of data or observations, either because it is much higher or much lower.

Knowledge check 25

How might a physicist show from Table 11, without plotting a graph, that the acceleration of a body subject to a constant force is inversely proportional to the body's mass?

Practical activity 5

Verification of the conservation of linear momentum in a collision

Background information

The linear momentum p of a moving object is the product of its mass and its velocity. Like velocity, momentum is a vector. One of the most important laws in physics is the law of conservation of linear momentum. This states that in the absence of external forces, the total momentum of a system before a collision is equal to the total momentum of that system after the collision.

This experiment is carried out on a linear air track of triangular cross-section. Air blowing through tiny holes in the track enables objects called gliders to move over the track without friction.

Practical activities

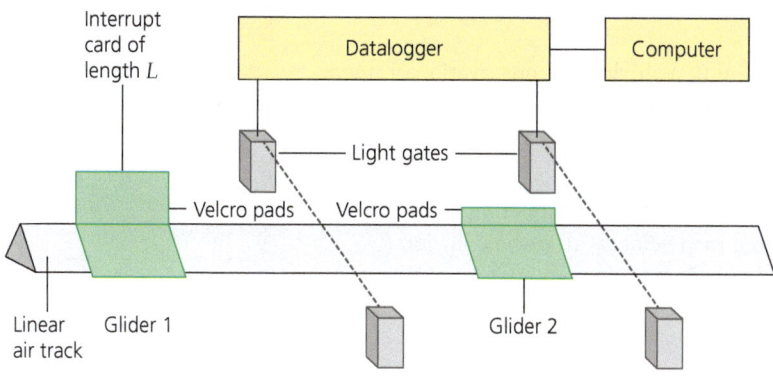

Figure 29 Linear air track

Practical procedure

1. The mass of glider 1 with its interrupt card (m_1), and glider 2 without an interrupt card (m_2) are found using a balance.
2. The length L of the interrupt card is measured using a ruler.
3. The apparatus is set up as shown in Figure 29. The air track is levelled and then connected to a blower.
4. With glider 2 stationary, give glider 1 a gentle push.
5. After collision, the two gliders coalesce at the Velcro pads and move off together.
6. Read the velocities of glider 1 (u) and the combined gliders (v) as they pass through the light gates.
7. Calculate the momentum before and after the collision, $p_{before} = m_1 u$ and $p_{after} = (m_1 + m_2)v$.
8. Repeat several times, with different velocities, and record the results in a prepared table.

Analysis of results

Typical results for this experiment are shown in Table 12.

Mass of glider $m_1 = 0.395$ kg. Mass of glider $m_2 = 0.405$ kg.

Table 12 Results of conservation of momentum experiment

Velocity of m_1/m s^{-1}	Momentum p_1 before collision/kg m s^{-1}	Velocity of combined gliders ($m_1 + m_2$)/m s^{-1}	Momentum p_2 after collision/kg m s^{-1}
0.25	0.10	0.13	0.10
0.32	0.13	0.17	0.14
0.45	0.18	0.23	0.18
0.55	0.22	0.28	0.22
0.60	0.24	0.30	0.24

The numbers in the second and fourth columns of the table demonstrate that, within the limits of experimental error, the momentum of glider 1 before the collision is equal to the combined momentum of the gliders after the collision. This agrees with the law of conservation of linear momentum.

Content Guidance

> **Worked example**
>
> a In the background information it was stated that the law of conservation of linear momentum is only valid in the absence of external forces. Give an example of one of the external forces which might be acting when two cars collide in a road traffic accident.
>
> b Using the data above, a student plotted a graph of the velocity of m_1 before the collision (u) (vertical axis) against the combined velocity after the collision (v). Describe the graph the student would obtain, justifying your answer with a suitable mapping.
>
> **Answer**
>
> a Friction between the tyres and the road (or friction in the brakes)
>
> b From the law of momentum conservation: $m_1 u = (m_1 + m_2)v$
>
> Dividing by m_1 gives: $u = \left(1 + \dfrac{m_2}{m_1}\right)v$
>
> Compare with the straight-line equation: $y = c + mx$
>
> The graph of u against v should therefore be a straight line through the origin of gradient $1 + \dfrac{m_2}{m_1}$.

> **Knowledge check 26**
>
> The incident momentum of a glider can be increased by pushing it harder. How else might this be achieved without increasing the speed?

> **Knowledge check 27**
>
> The unit for momentum in the table is given as $kg\,m\,s^{-1}$. Some books quote the unit as $N\,s$. Demonstrate that the two units are the same.

Refinement

The experimental method covers only one type of collision called a completely inelastic collision, in which the kinetic energy after the collision is very much less than that before the collision. A complete treatment would require investigation of almost elastic collisions (where the colliding gliders do not coalesce) and super-elastic (explosive) collisions (where a concealed spring pushes apart two gliders which are initially at rest).

A note on Newton's second law

Practical activity 4 established the equation $F = ma$. Practical activity 5 was a study on what happens to momentum when one body produces a force on another as a result of a collision. The two ideas are closely linked.

$$F = ma = m\frac{v - u}{t} = \frac{mv - mu}{t}$$

$$= \frac{\text{change in momentum}}{\text{time}}$$

$$= \text{rate of change of momentum}$$

In his original work, Newton expressed what is now known as Newton's second law ($F = ma$) in terms of momentum.

Practical activity 6

Investigate the energy exchange between potential and kinetic for a falling body

Background information

The gravitational potential energy E_p of a mass m is given by the equation:

$E_p = mgh$

Practical activities

where g is the gravitational field strength and h is the height above a given reference point, often taken as the Earth's surface. In this experiment its kinetic energy E_k is given by:

$$E_k = \frac{1}{2}mv^2$$

where v is its velocity.

If an object accelerates towards the Earth's surface, its height decreases and so does its gravitational potential energy. However, its kinetic energy increases because its velocity increases. This experiment seeks to demonstrate that the amount of gravitational energy lost is equal to the amount of kinetic energy gained, that is, the total energy of the falling object is constant.

Practical procedure

The apparatus used is the same as that in the experiment to find the acceleration of free fall.

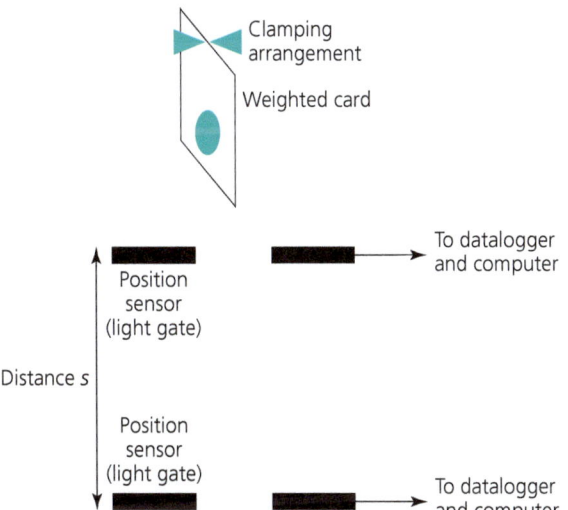

Figure 30 Arrangement for energy conservation experiment

1. The mass of the weighted card is first found using a balance and the apparatus is assembled as shown in Figure 30.
2. Start with the distance s set at about 1 m and the lower end of the card as close to the upper light gate as possible.
3. The length of the card is entered into the datalogger, so that the equipment can calculate its velocity as it passes each light gate.
4. These velocities are found three times and means recorded.
5. The distance s is then increased in steps of 50 cm and the experiment repeated for each value of s.
6. The whole experiment should be repeated for different masses.

Analysis of results

With care, you might obtain results (for a single mass) similar to those shown in Table 13.

> **Knowledge check 28**
> Why is it important that the distance between the light gates is as large as conveniently possible?

Content Guidance

Mass of weighted card = 0.050 kg

Table 13 Data for energy conservation experiment

Distance s/m	Velocity at upper light gate/m s⁻¹	Velocity at lower light gate/m s⁻¹	Gain in kinetic energy/J	Loss in GPE (= mgs)/J
1.00	0.50	4.46	0.49	0.49
1.50	0.49	5.44	0.73	0.74
2.00	0.50	6.28	0.98	0.98
2.50	0.51	7.02	1.23	1.23

The critical two columns are those on the right-hand side of the table, which demonstrate that, for a falling body of this mass, the loss in gravitational potential energy is equal to the increase in kinetic energy.

> **Worked example**
>
> This experiment has been done on the Moon using a mass of 50 g. In what way (if at all) would the results be **a** different and **b** the same when compared with those in Table 13?
>
> **Answer**
>
> **a** Different: The velocities at each light gate would all have been smaller because the acceleration of free fall on the Moon is only about a sixth of that on Earth. Hence, the numbers in the 2nd, 3rd, 4th and 5th columns of the table would all have been smaller.
>
> **b** Same: At each distance the gain in kinetic energy would have been the same as the loss in gravitational potential energy.

> **Knowledge check 29**
>
> There are several different conservation laws in physics.
>
> **a** Which conservation law is illustrated by this experiment?
>
> **b** Name two other important conservation laws.

Practical activity 7

Determine resistance by the ammeter–voltmeter method and using a multimeter or ohmmeter and the *I–V* characteristics of a metallic conductor at constant temperature and a filament lamp

Background information

The resistance R of an electrical component is defined as the ratio of the voltage across it, V, to the current flowing through it, I. Expressed mathematically, $R = \frac{V}{I}$. Electrical resistance is always measured in units called ohms (symbol Ω).

The resistance of most materials changes with temperature. This is true, for example, of metal wires, filaments in electrical lamps, thermistors and semiconductors. The experiment being described here relates to the resistance of a piece of nichrome wire.

> **Knowledge check 30**
>
> Electrical resistance R is defined by $R = \frac{V}{I}$. Does this mean the wire has no resistance when there is no voltage across it?

Practical procedure: multimeter (or ohmmeter) method

Multimeters are capable of measuring many electrical quantities (Figure 31). Even the most inexpensive can measure current, voltage and resistance. Any meter capable of measuring electrical resistance is simply called an ohmmeter. The big advantage of using a multimeter is the speed with which the resistance can be found. It is also no less accurate than the ammeter–voltmeter method. The second big advantage of using a digital multimeter is that they are often internally protected from overloading. Often the worst that can happen is the multimeter will blow a fuse. On the other hand, overloading an analogue (moving coil) meter can cause irreparable damage.

The first task of the user is to select what is to be measured by the multimeter, often by using a rotary selector switch on the face of the instrument. Figure 32 shows such a selector. The arrow on the bar is pointing to a symbol which shows that this multimeter is set to check electrical continuity. If the multimeter is to be used to measure electrical resistance, the switch must be turned clockwise to, say, 200 Ω. The two leads connected to the multimeter are then connected across the device being tested and the multimeter is switched on. If the resistance is less than 200 Ω, its value will appear on the display.

If the resistance is greater than 200 Ω, the multimeter display will show an overflow condition, often indicated by a single numerical 1 on the display. You should switch it off, set a new range with the selector, switch the multimeter on again and continue as before.

Figure 31 Analogue and digital multimeters

Practical procedure: ammeter–voltmeter method

The apparatus required for this method is:

- low voltage power supply unit (PSU) or 6 V battery
- rheostat
- ammeter
- voltmeter
- connecting leads
- resistance wire
- switch

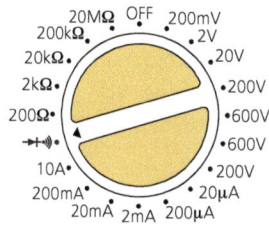

Figure 32 A multimeter selector switch

1. Prepare a table for your results, such as Table 14.
2. Set up the circuit as shown in Figure 33.
3. Adjust the PSU to supply to zero volts and then switch it on.
4. Record the voltage on the voltmeter and the corresponding current on the ammeter.
5. Switch off the PSU and allow the wire to cool to room temperature.
6. Switch on the PSU again and adjust the voltage so that the voltmeter reading increases by 1 V.
7. Repeat for voltages from zero to a maximum voltage of 5 V. This is Trial 1.
8. Repeat the entire experiment to obtain a second set of current values. This is Trial 2.

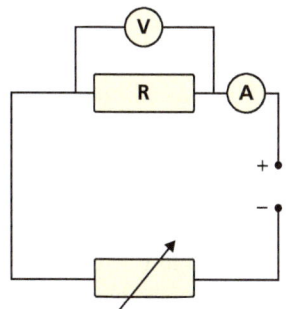

Figure 33 Circuit to find the electrical resistance of *R*

Analysis of results

A careful experimentalist might obtain a set of results like those in Table 14.

Table 14 Typical experimental results

Voltage *V*/V	0.00	1.00	2.00	3.00	4.00	5.00
(Trial 1) Current/A	0.00	0.21	0.38	0.60	0.80	0.96
(Trial 2) Current/A	0.00	0.19	0.42	0.60	0.79	0.94

Content Guidance

Worked example

a Complete the fourth row of the table by calculating the mean current from the two trials.
b Use your answers from part a to calculate the resistance at each voltage.
c Suggest a reason why the resistance at 5.00 V appears to be slightly larger than the others.

Answer

a and **b**

Mean current I_{mean}/A	0.00	0.20	0.40	0.60	0.80	0.95
Resistance R/Ω	—	5.00	5.00	5.00	5.00	5.26

c The current is now big enough to cause heating in the wire – so the temperature is rising.

Refinement

All ammeter–voltmeter methods to find resistance have an inherent problem. To operate, a small current must flow through the voltmeter. But this means that the current measured on the ammeter is not the same as that flowing through the resistor. The problem is minimised by using digital voltmeters. They have an extremely high internal resistance so that the current drawn away from the resistor is very, very small indeed.

Practical procedure: *I–V* characteristic of the metal wire

The data collected enable us to plot a graph of mean current against voltage for this piece of resistance wire. This graph should be a straight line through the origin. It is the first quadrant part of the *I–V* characteristic. To obtain the other part of the characteristic, we must repeat the experiment after reversing the polarity on the PSU. This will cause the readings on the digital meters to change from positive to negative values. Plotting these values will give us the third quadrant part of the graph and complete the characteristic, as shown in Figure 34.

Practical procedure: *I–V* characteristic of a filament lamp

The procedure and results table for this experiment are almost identical to those for the metal wire. The differences are:

1 A 6 V filament lamp (torch bulb) is used instead of a piece of resistance wire.
2 There is no need to switch off between readings to allow the filament to cool down. The filament reaches its working temperature again shortly after switching on.

The circuit diagram is shown in Figure 35.

Knowledge check 32

An electric current is best described as the flow of electrons in a conductor. In which direction do they flow?

Exam tip

If you are required to construct an electrical circuit, leave the addition of the voltmeter to the end. Once the rest has been set up, check that a current flows in the ammeter when the PSU is switched on. Only if the rest of the circuit is working should you add the voltmeter. A logical approach like this makes fault finding much simpler.

Knowledge check 31

The procedure for this experiment involves adjusting the voltage across the resistance wire. With reference to Figure 34, state how this is done.

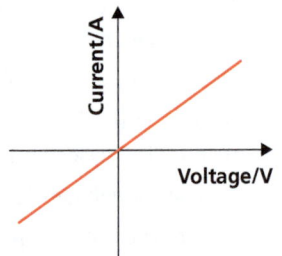

Figure 34 *I–V* characteristic for a metal wire

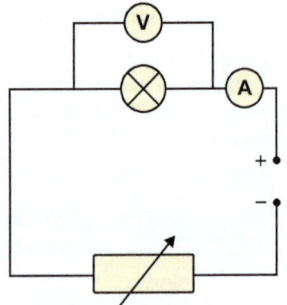

Figure 35 Circuit used to find the *I–V* characteristic of a filament lamp

Practical activities

Analysis of results

Why is the *I–V* characteristic of a filament lamp a curve of decreasing gradient (Figure 36), while that of a metal wire is a straight line through the origin? The first thing to notice is that a metal wire at constant temperature has a constant resistance. This is demonstrated in Table 14.

However, for the filament lamp, the *I–V* characteristic is a curve of decreasing gradient. This tells us that the resistance of the filament is increasing as the current increases. The difference here is that the temperature of the wire is allowed to rise. We know this because we see the wire glows with a low current and then as the current increases it gets whiter and whiter as its temperature rises.

So, the resistance of the filament is strongly linked to its temperature. To understand why, we need to remember that an electric current is simply the flow of electrons around a circuit. As they do so, they collide with vibrating atoms in the metal lattice. It is these collisions which give rise to the property of electrical resistance.

If now the temperature rises, the atoms in the lattice vibrate with increasing amplitude and the collision frequency with the conduction electrons increases. This increased collision frequency gives rise to increased electrical resistance.

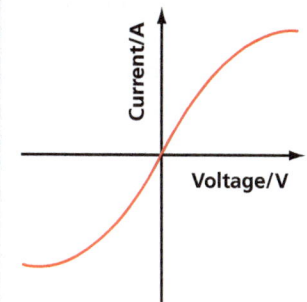

Figure 36 *I–V* characteristic of a filament lamp

> **Exam tip**
>
> Some students mistakenly believe that electrical resistance is the gradient of the *V–I* graph. It is not. Resistance is the instantaneous voltage divided by the instantaneous current, not the rate of change of voltage with current.

Practical activity 8

Verify the relationships for resistors in (a) series and (b) parallel

Background information

The combined resistance R of resistors $R_1, R_2, R_3, \ldots, R_n$ in series is given by the formula:

$$R_{series} = R_1 + R_2 + R_3 + \ldots + R_n$$

The combined resistance R of resistors $R_1, R_2, R_3, \ldots, R_n$ in parallel is given by the formula:

$$R^{-1}{}_{parallel} = R_1^{-1} + R_2^{-1} + R_3^{-1} + \ldots + R_n^{-1}$$

This experiment seeks to verify these two formulae experimentally using a multimeter as an ohmmeter.

Practical procedure

The equipment required for both experiments is:
- a multimeter capable of reading up to $500\,\Omega$
- assorted resistors, each between $50\,\Omega$ and $100\,\Omega$
- connecting wire

The school or college technician should determine the resistance of each resistor with the multimeter and attach a sticky label showing its resistance to each. This can be done before the experiment is carried out.

Series arrangements

An arrangement of two resistors in series is connected across the multimeter and the resistance of R_1, R_2 and the total resistance are recorded in a table like

Table 15. Similarly, an arrangement of three (and four) resistors in series (Figure 37) is connected across the multimeter and the resistance of R_1, R_2, R_3 (and R_4) and the total resistance are recorded in the table.

Table 15 Typical results for series arrangements

No. of resistors	R_1/Ω	R_2/Ω	R_3/Ω	R_4/Ω	Total resistance R/Ω
2	51	77			128
3	51	77	62		190
4	51	77	62	60	250

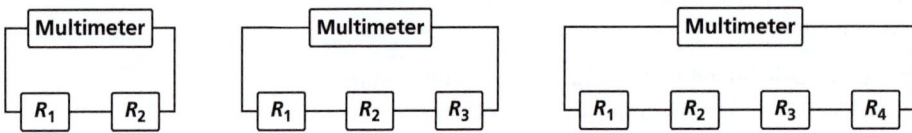

Figure 37 Two, three and four resistors in series across a multimeter

Notice from Table 15 that the experimental results confirm the equation:

$$R_{series} = R_1 + R_2 + R_3 + \ldots + R_n$$

Parallel arrangements

Two, three and four resistors can also be arranged in parallel with each other and each arrangement connected across the multimeter. As before, the resistance of each resistor and the total resistance of the arrangement are recorded. Typical results are shown in Table 16.

The experiment can naturally be extended for five or more resistors in series or parallel.

Table 16 Typical results for parallel arrangements

No. of resistors	R_1/Ω	R_2/Ω	R_3/Ω	R_4/Ω	R_1^{-1}/Ω^{-1}	R_2^{-1}/Ω^{-1}	R_3^{-1}/Ω^{-1}	R_4^{-1}/Ω^{-1}	$(R_1^{-1} + R_2^{-1} + R_3^{-1} + R_4^{-1})^{-1}/\Omega$	$R_{parallel}/\Omega$
2	51	77			0.020	0.013			30.3	30.7
3	51	77	62		0.020	0.013	0.016		20.4	20.5
4	51	77	62	60	0.020	0.013	0.016	0.017	15.2	15.3

Notice from Table 16 that the experimental results confirm the equation:

$$R^{-1}_{parallel} = R_1^{-1} + R_2^{-1} + R_3^{-1} + \ldots + R_n^{-1}$$

> **Worked example**
>
> A student carried out the experiment outlined above to investigate the relationships for resistances in series and parallel.
>
> **a** Verify from the student's data in Table 15 that for resistors in series:
>
> $$R_{series} = R_1 + R_2 + R_3 + \ldots + R_n$$
>
> **b** Verify from the student's data in Table 16 that for resistors in parallel:
>
> $$R^{-1}_{parallel} = R_1^{-1} + R_2^{-1} + R_3^{-1} + \ldots + R_n^{-1}$$

Answer

a Consider each row in turn:

For two resistors: total resistance $R = R_1 + R_2 = 51 + 77 = 128$ (right-hand column)

For three resistors: total resistance $R = R_1 + R_2 + R_3 = 51 + 77 + 62 = 190$ (right-hand column)

For four resistors: total resistance $R = R_1 + R_2 + R_3 + R_4 = 51 + 77 + 62 + 60 = 250$ (right-hand column)

By extension therefore: $R_{series} = R_1 + R_2 + R_3 + \ldots + R_n$

If $R_1 = R_2 = R_3 = \ldots = R_n = R$, then $R_{series} = R + R + R + \ldots + R = n \times R$

b Consider each row in turn and compare the last two results columns on the left-hand side:

For two resistors: $30.3 \approx 30.7$ so $R^{-1}_{parallel} \approx R_1^{-1} + R_2^{-1}$

For three resistors: $20.4 \approx 20.5$ so $R^{-1}_{parallel} \approx R_1^{-1} + R_2^{-1} + R_3^{-1}$

For four resistors: $15.2 \approx 15.3$ so $R^{-1}_{parallel} \approx R_1^{-1} + R_2^{-1} + R_3^{-1} + R_4^{-1}$

These are experimental results, so within the limits of experimental error we can write:

By extension: $R^{-1}_{parallel} = R_1^{-1} + R_2^{-1} + R_3^{-1} + \ldots + R_n^{-1}$

Practical activity 9

Determine the resistivity of a material

Background information

The resistivity of a material ρ is defined by the equation $\rho = \frac{R \times A}{L}$, where R is the material's resistance, A is its cross-section area and L is its length. It therefore has units $\Omega\,m$. Good conductors (such as copper) have a low resistivity (around $1.7 \times 10^{-8}\,\Omega\,m$) while good insulators (such as PTFE (Teflon)) have a high resistivity (around $10^{23}\,\Omega\,m$).

This experiment involves the measurement of the resistivity of the material in a piece of nichrome wire, about a metre long and about 0.3 mm in diameter. Nichrome is an alloy of nickel, chromium and iron.

In this experiment, the ammeter–voltmeter method is preferable to using an ohmmeter to measure resistance. This is because the resistance of the wire is so small, typically a few ohms. The resistance is found from the equation $R = \frac{V}{I}$.

Mapping the equation $R = \frac{\rho \times L}{A}$ to the equation of a straight line, we see that a graph of R (vertical axis) against L (horizontal axis) should produce a straight line through the origin of gradient $\frac{\rho}{A}$. If we then find the cross-section area and the gradient of the straight line, we can calculate the resistivity as their product.

Practical procedure

1 Set up the circuit shown in Figure 38.

2 Using the ammeter–voltmeter method, determine the resistance of different lengths L of nichrome wire ranging from about 10 cm to about 90 cm.

> **Exam tip**
> Sometimes examiners ask students to calculate the resistance of a network involving both series and parallel combinations. It is useful to remember that the combined resistance of any two resistors in parallel is their product divided by their sum.

> **Exam tip**
> The equation for resistors in parallel begins '$R^{-1}_{parallel} = \ldots$'. The standard error made by students when asked to find the total resistance of a parallel network is to forget to take the final reciprocal. Remember $R_{parallel} = (R^{-1}_{parallel})^{-1}$.

> **Knowledge check 33**
> Explain why the total resistance of the circuit decreases as more and more resistors are connected in parallel across the battery.

Content Guidance

3 Record the results in a pre-prepared table.
4 Plot the graph of resistance R against length L and determine its gradient.
5 Measure the diameter of the wire at about six different places along its length using a micrometer and hence determine the mean cross-section area A using $A = \frac{\pi \times d^2}{4}$.
6 Determine the resistivity of the nichrome by calculating the product of the gradient and the mean cross-section area (csa).

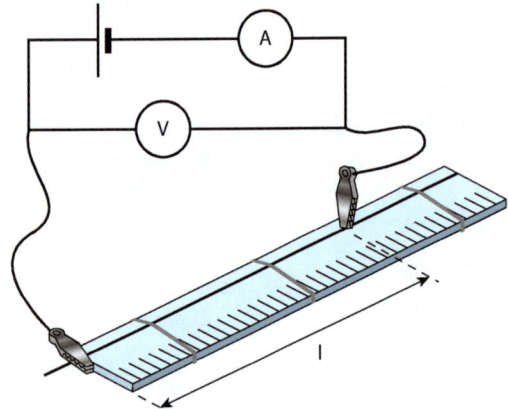

Figure 38 Experiment to measure resistivity

Safety

Although the voltages being measured are small, care should be taken to prevent short circuits. This is particularly important in those schools and colleges where mains-powered low-voltage PSUs are used.

Analysis of results

A typical set of results for this experiment, showing the micrometer readings and the graph of resistance against length, is given in Figure 39.

Diameter of the wire D/mm = 0.31, 0.30, 0.39, 0.32, 0.33, 0.34

Mean diameter $d = 0.32$ mm

$A = \frac{\pi \times d^2}{4} = 8.04 \times 10^{-8}\,\text{m}^2$

Gradient of graph = $14\,\Omega\,\text{m}^{-1}$

Resistivity = gradient × csa = $1.13 \times 10^{-6}\,\Omega\,\text{m}$

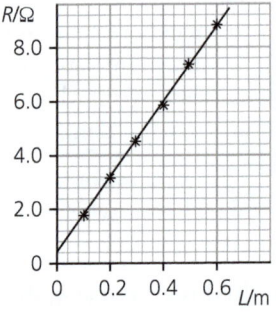

Figure 39 Resistance versus length graph in resisitivity experiment

Worked example

A student working beside you obtains the following data when working with a length of resistance wire. However, the student who obtained the results does not know how to use them to determine the resistivity of the resistance wire. Plot the appropriate graph, provide the appropriate analysis and carry out the necessary calculations to show her how to determine the resistivity.

Diameter/mm: 0.51, 0.49, 0.50, 0.61, 0.51, 0.49

Length/m	0.20	0.40	0.60	0.80	1.00
Resistance/Ω	0.50	1.00	1.50	2.00	2.50

Answer

Since $\rho = \dfrac{R \times A}{L}$, the resistivity is the product of the gradient of the graph of resistance against length and the cross-section area (Figure 40).

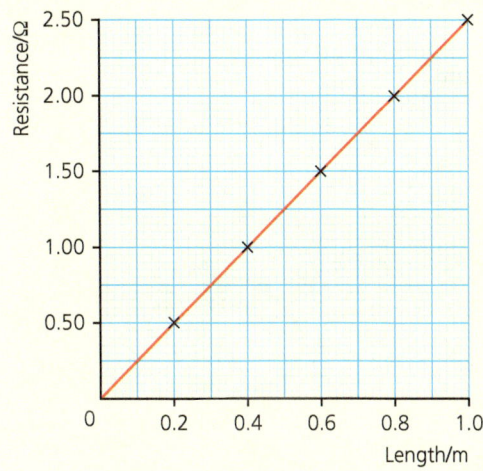

Figure 40 Graph of resistance versus length

Gradient = $\dfrac{\text{rise}}{\text{run}} = \dfrac{2.50}{1.00} = 2.50\,\Omega\,\text{m}^{-1}$

Mean diameter = $\dfrac{0.51 + 0.49 + 0.50 + 0.51 + 0.49}{5} = 0.50\,\text{mm}$

(The 0.61 mm measurement is an outlier and is disregarded.)

Cross-section area = $\dfrac{\pi \times d^2}{4} = 1.96 \times 10^{-7}\,\text{m}^2$

Resistivity = gradient × csa = $2.50 \times 1.96 \times 10^{-7}$

$= 4.9 \times 10^{-7}\,\Omega\,\text{m}$

> **Exam tip**
>
> Using a micrometer is an essential skill for the A-level physics student. The only way to learn the skill is to practise using it. Practise, practise, practise.

> **Knowledge check 34**
>
> The range of resistivities of natural materials is enormous. Of what orders of magnitude are the resistivities of the best conductors and the best insulators?

Practical activity 10

Determine the resistance–temperature characteristic of a negative temperature coefficient (ntc) thermistor

Background information

The resistance of metals increases with rising temperature. However, there is a class of materials, known as negative temperature coefficient (ntc) semiconductors, in which the resistance decreases as the temperature increases. Such materials are used to make devices called thermistors.

The purpose of this experiment is to investigate how the resistance of a thermistor changes with changing temperature and to plot the resistance–temperature graph (known as the characteristic).

Content Guidance

Practical procedure

1. The thermistor is mounted in a large beaker and connected to an ammeter–voltmeter arrangement to determine its resistance, as shown in Figure 41.
2. When all is set up, boiling water is poured into the beaker.
3. A liquid-in-glass thermometer is used to measure the temperature around the thermistor.
4. At the same time, readings are taken of current and voltage, in order to determine the thermistor's resistance.
5. Step 4 is repeated at various temperatures as the water cools and the results are recorded as in Table 17.

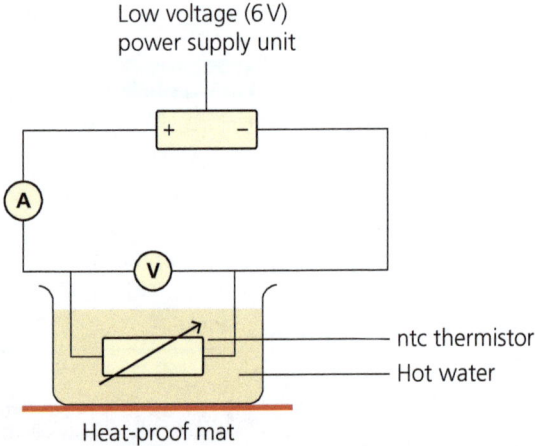

Figure 41 Apparatus to investigate how thermistor resistance changes with temperature

Table 17 Typical results in ntc thermistor experiment

Temperature/°C	90	80	70	60	50	40	30	20
Voltage/V	6.0	6.0	6.0	6.0	6.0	6.0	6.0	6.0
Current/mA	220	170	120	90	70	50	40	30
Resistance/Ω	27	35	50	67	86	120	150	200

Worked example

a Use the data in Table 17 to plot the resistance–temperature characteristic for the thermistor.

b Use the characteristic to predict the temperature at which the thermistor's resistance is 180 Ω.

Exam tip

Take care when using submultiple units such as milliamperes (mA) when doing calculations. Remember 1 mA = 0.001 A. When finding resistance in ohms, the current should first be converted to amperes.

Practical activities

Answer

a

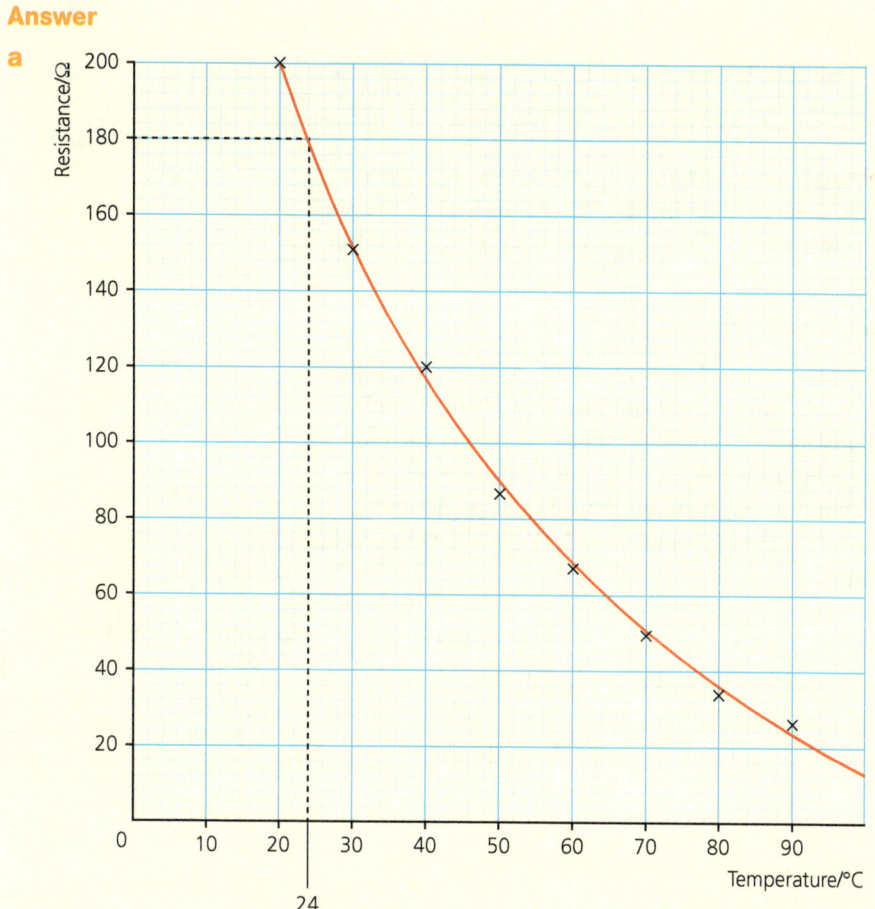

Figure 42 NTC thermistor characteristic curve

b From the graph, the temperature at which the thermistor's resistance is 180 Ω is 24 °C.

Analysis of results

The experiment demonstrates that resistance of an ntc thermistor decreases rapidly with increasing temperature. At any given voltage, the increase in temperature, and with it thermal energy, causes a significant increase in the number of conducting electrons and so an increased current in the circuit. This in turn is observed as a reduction in the electrical resistance.

> **Knowledge check 35**
>
> The thermistor characteristic in Figure 42 may touch the vertical axis but will never touch the horizontal axis. Explain why not.

Practical techniques and data analysis

Content Guidance

Practical activity 11
Determine the e.m.f. and internal resistance of a battery

Background information
When there is a current I in an electric cell, the terminal p.d. V is less than the e.m.f. E of the cell because work has to be done overcoming the internal resistance r of the cell. This can be expressed by the equation: $V = E - Ir$. This equation is provided in the data sheet for CCEA examinations.

Rearranging the equation for e.m.f. gives: $V = -rI + E$.

Mapping with the general equation of a straight line, $y = mx + c$, shows that a graph of V on the y-axis against I on the x-axis will be a straight line of gradient $-r$ and intercept E (provided the internal resistance is constant). The experiment therefore involves measuring the terminal p.d. for different values of current in the cell. The simplest experiment is to do this for a dry cell, such as a 1.5 V D cell (sometimes called an R20 cell). Perhaps surprisingly, the experiment works best when the cell has been used and is partially discharged.

Practical procedure
1. Set up the circuit arrangement shown in Figure 43.
2. Verify that, as the resistance of the variable resistor is increased, the current drawn from the cell decreases and the terminal p.d., as shown on the voltmeter, increases.
3. For different settings of the rheostat, record in a pre-prepared table the voltage on the voltmeter and the current on the milliammeter, for currents ranging from 500 mA down to about 100 mA.

Safety
The following safety precautions should be observed:
- Although low voltages are being used, care should be taken with the wiring to prevent a short circuit.
- Digital meters should be handled with care and suitable scales selected to minimise the risk of damage.

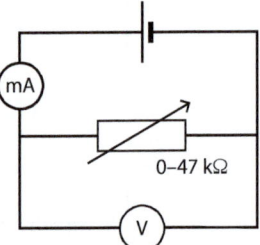

Figure 43 Measuring the e.m.f. and internal resistance of a cell

A typical set of results is shown in Table 18 and Figure 44.

Table 18 Typical results in e.m.f. experiment

I/mA	100	150	200	250	300	350	400	450	500
V/V	1.44	1.41	1.38	1.35	1.32	1.29	1.26	1.23	1.20

Practical activities

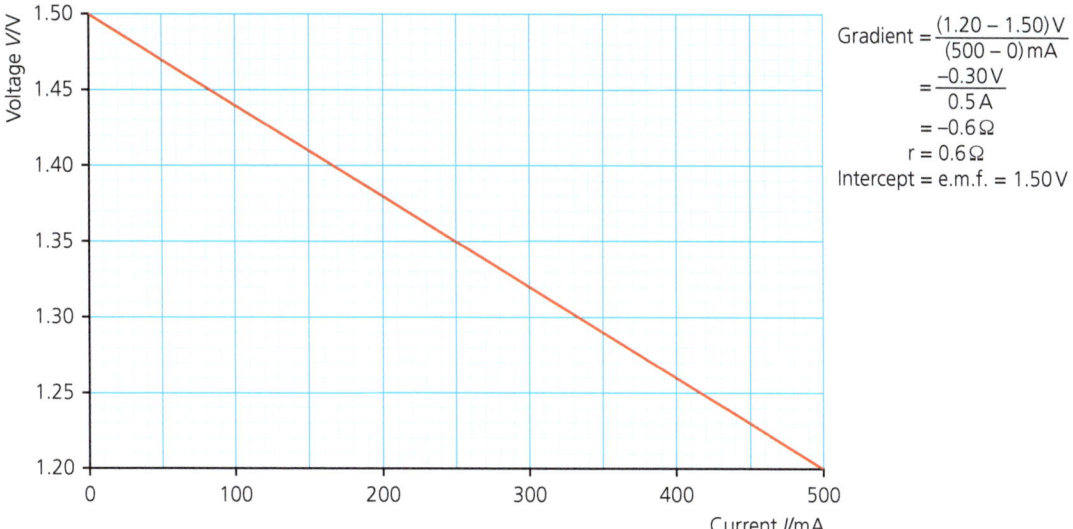

Figure 44 Graph to find e.m.f. and internal resistance

Worked example

a A 22 Ω rotary potentiometer was used for the variable resistor. Use the data in the table to explain why this is a suitable choice.
b What is the control variable that must remain constant in this experiment?
c By mistake a student plots a graph of I/A (on the vertical axis) against V/V (on the horizontal axis). By rearranging the equation $V = E - rI$ to make I the subject and mapping it to the equation of a straight line, state how the student could use the graph to find the internal resistance and the e.m.f. of the cell.
d The graph in Figure 44 does not start from a (0, 0) origin. Suggest why the vertical axis starts from 1.20 V, but the horizontal axis stars from 0 mA.
e Why is it important to use a voltmeter of high internal resistance?

Answer

a When $I = 100$ mA, $V = 1.44$ V, so $R = V/I = 1.44\,V/0.1\,A = 14.4\,\Omega$.
When $I = 500$ mA, $V = 1.20$ V, so $R = V/I = 1.20\,V/0.5\,A = 2.40\,\Omega$.
The resistance needs to have a range from 2.40 Ω to 14.4 Ω.
Therefore, a 22 Ω rotary potentiometer, which can be varied from 0 to 22 Ω, will be suitable. The cell's e.m.f. must not change throughout the experiment.
b The e.m.f. is the control variable.
c $V = E - rI$, so $I = \dfrac{E}{r} - \dfrac{1}{r} \times V$
Comparing with $y = c + mx$, the gradient is $-\dfrac{1}{r}$, so $r = -1/\text{gradient}$.
The intercept (after extrapolation) on the vertical axis is $\dfrac{E}{r}$, so $E = r \times \text{intercept}$.
d That part of the graph below 1.20 V is not required. Starting from 1.20 V allows a much larger scale on the vertical axis. It is essential that the horizontal axis starts at 0 mA if the point where the graph cuts the vertical axis is the intercept $(0, E)$.
e A voltmeter should draw the minimum current from the circuit of which it is a part. Otherwise the voltage to be measured drops. This is the reason why digital meters are superior to analogue moving-coil meters for this experiment. All but the cheapest digital voltmeters have a very high internal resistance.

Exam tip

Your plotted points should occupy at least half the space available and you should label the axes exactly as the headings appear in the table.

Knowledge check 36

Eight 1.5 V dry cells in series produce a 12 V battery. From your knowledge of internal resistance, suggest why such a battery could not be used to start a car engine.

Exam tip

Always look carefully at the axes labels given on a graph. In a recent paper, a graph showed the current on the vertical axis and the voltage on the horizontal axis, requiring students to undertake a mapping exercise, rather than rely on their memory.

Content Guidance

Practical activity 12
Verify Snell's law and determine the refractive index of a material

Background information
- Refraction is the change in the direction of a beam of light as it travels from one material into another. It occurs because light travels at different speeds in different materials (Figure 45).
- Light travels slower in optically dense materials (such as glass) and faster in optically rare materials like air.
- Light slows down when it leaves the air and enters glass, so it bends towards the **normal**.
- Light speeds up when it leaves the glass and re-enters the air, so it bends away from the normal.

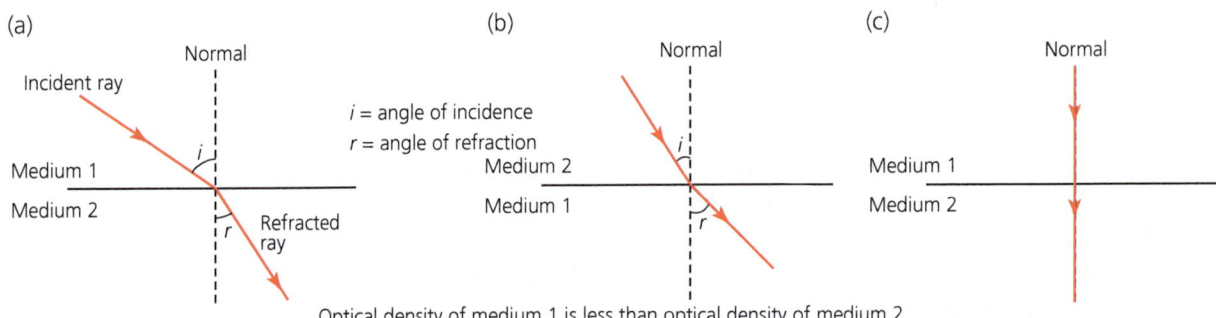

Figure 45 The behaviour of light in refraction

Snell's law and refractive index

Snell's law states that the ratio of the sine of the **angle of incidence** to the sine of the **angle of refraction** is the same for all rays travelling across a given boundary. This means that the ratio $\sin i / \sin r$ is a constant for any two given media. This ratio for the boundary between any two particular media is also equal to the **refractive index**, denoted by the symbol n.

The aim of this experiment is to verify Snell's law and to determine the refractive index for the material in a transparent, rectangular block (usually glass or an acrylic such as Perspex®).

Practical procedure
1. Place the rectangular glass block on a sheet of white paper and draw around its outline with a sharp pencil (Figure 46).
2. Remove the block and draw a normal near the middle of one of the longer sides of the block.
3. Use a protractor to draw a line representing an incident ray at an angle of incidence i of 30°.
4. Replace the block on its outline on the paper.
5. Place the ray box to direct a ray of light along the line drawn.

Normal A line drawn at right angles to a surface.

Angle of incidence The angle between the incident ray and the normal to the boundary of a transparent material.

Angle of refraction The angle between the refracted ray and the normal to the boundary of a transparent material.

Refractive index The ratio of the sine of the angle of incidence to the sine of the angle of refraction.

Practical activities

6 Mark the path of the emergent ray.
7 Remove the block and join the points of incidence and emergence with a straight line to construct the path of the ray through the block.
8 Repeat this procedure for angles of incidence i of 40°, 50°, 60° and 70° using the same normal line.
9 Record the data in a table.

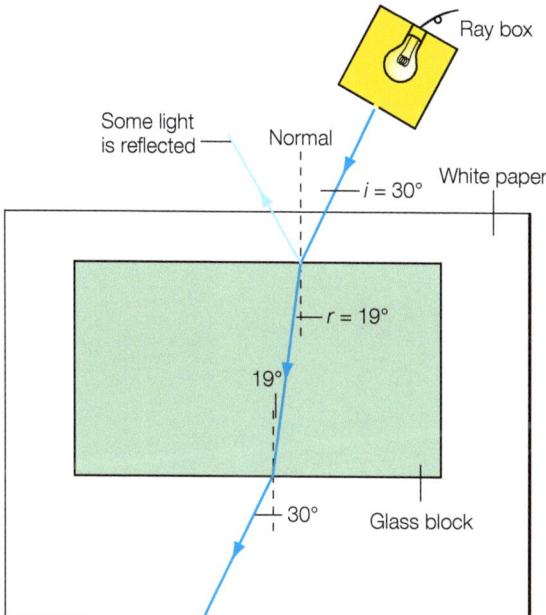

Figure 46 Experimental arrangement for Snell's law

Worked example

A student carries out the method above and records the results in Table 19. One way of treating the experimental data is simply to calculate the ratio $\frac{\sin i}{\sin r}$. The constancy of this ratio is adequate evidence to verify Snell's law. The mean value of the ratio (in this case it is 1.51) is the best value to accept as the refractive index. However, the student decides to take the approach of plotting a graph to calculate the refractive index.

Table 19 Typical results that might be achieved by a careful student

Angle of incidence $i/°$	30	40	50	60	70
Angle of refraction $r/°$	19	25	31	35	39
$\sin i/°$	0.500	0.643	0.766	0.866	0.940
$\sin r/°$	0.326	0.423	0.515	0.574	0.629
$n = \sin(i/°)/\sin(r/°)$	1.53	1.52	1.49	1.51	1.49

a How should the student rearrange Snell's law to map their results to a straight line?
b Using the data in Table 19, plot the straight-line graph according to your answer in part a.
c Calculate the refractive index from your graph

> **Exam tip**
> When drawing rays of light on a diagram always show the direction in which the light is travelling with an arrow.

> **Exam tip**
> Always be careful to give units in tables and on graph axes. Note that in this experiment i and r are in degrees, but the values of $\sin i$ and $\sin r$ are dimensionless. That is why the brackets are essential.

Content Guidance

Answer

a Snell's law gives $n = \dfrac{\sin(i/°)}{\sin(r/°)}$

Rearranging gives $\sin i = n \times \sin r$.

Comparing this with the straight-line equation $y = mx + c$, we see the gradient m corresponds to n and $c = 0$.

If a graph is plotted of $\sin i$ on the y-axis against $\sin r$ on the x-axis, a straight-line graph through the origin will verify Snell's law (Figure 47).

The gradient of the straight line is equal to the refractive index of glass n.

Note that Table 19 shows the angles of incidence and refraction measured to the nearest degree. While this is usually the case, some protractors are capable of measuring angles with a resolution of 0.5°.

b

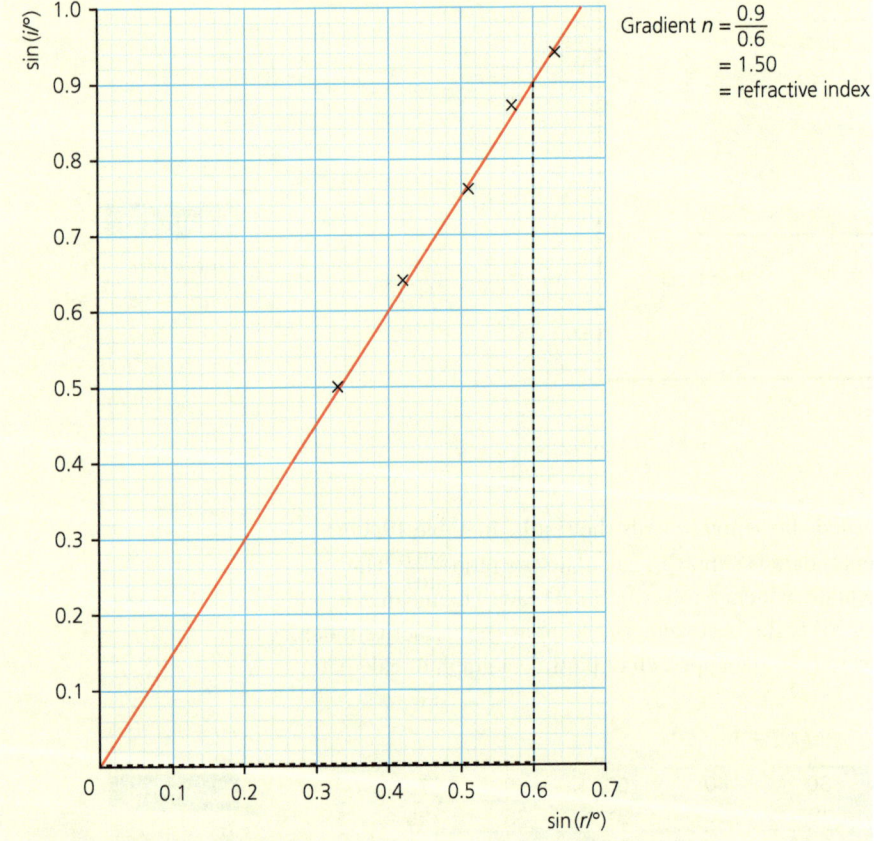

Figure 47 Graph to verify Snell's law and find the refractive index

c Refractive index = 1.50

> **Knowledge check 37**
>
> What is the relationship between the refractive index and the speed of light in air and in glass?

Practical activities

Practical activity 13
Determine the critical angle of glass or Perspex® using a semicircular block

Background information

When light travels from glass into air it bends away from the normal, but at the same time a weak internally reflected ray is observed. As the angle of incidence in glass increases, the refracted ray becomes weaker and the internally reflected ray becomes stronger, until a very weak refracted ray is observed with a large angle of refraction.

The angle of incidence in glass that results in an angle of refraction in air of 90° is called the **critical angle**, c. The critical angle for glass is typically around 42°.

At angles of incidence above the critical angle there is no refraction. The light is totally internally reflected.

Critical angle The angle of incidence in an optically dense medium when the angle of refraction in air is 90°.

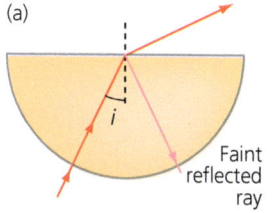
(a)
Faint reflected ray
Angle of incidence is **less** than the critical angle
Most of the light *passes through* into the air, but a little bit is *internally reflected*

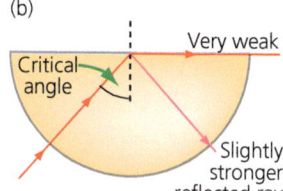
(b)
Critical angle
Very weak
Slightly stronger reflected ray
Angle of incidence is **equal** to the critical angle
The emerging ray comes out *along the surface*. There is quite a bit of *internal reflection*

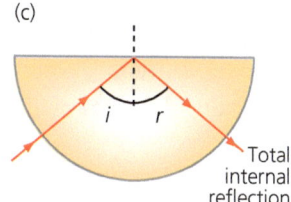
(c)
Total internal reflection
Angle of incidence is **greater** than the critical angle
No light is refracted
It is *all* internally reflected, i.e. *total internal reflection*

Figure 48 Changes in the angle of incidence in glass

The aim of this experiment is to determine the critical angle of glass using a semicircular glass block.

Practical procedure

1. Place the semicircular glass block on a sheet of white paper and draw round its outline with a sharp pencil.
2. Remove the block, mark the centre X of the straight diameter and then replace the block.
3. Switch on the PSU and direct a ray of light from a ray box towards X.
4. Ensure the angle of incidence in glass is small so that the refracted ray at X is clearly seen, as in Figure 48(a).
5. Continue to direct the ray towards X, but slowly move the ray box so that the angle at X increases and observe that the internally reflected ray becomes stronger.
6. Continue to move the ray box to increase the angle of incidence at X, until the refracted ray just emerges along the diameter, as in Figure 48(b).

Content Guidance

7   Observe that if the angle of incidence is now increased, even slightly, the light is totally internally reflected, as in Figure 48(c).
8   With a pencil, draw on the paper two dots on the incident ray as far apart from each other as possible and then remove the glass block. Join the dots on the incident ray using a pencil and ruler and extend the line beyond the point of incidence to X.
9   With a protractor draw the normal to the diameter at X and measure the critical angle c.
10 Record the value in a table.
11 Repeat the entire experiment about four more times and calculate the mean value obtained for the critical angle.

> **Knowledge check 38**
>
> Explain why there is no bending of the light at the curved surface of the semicircular glass block and use your answer to state the angle of incidence at the curved surface of the semicircular glass block.

Worked example

The experiment generally shows the average value of the critical angle to be 41.8°.

a Use this value to determine the refractive index of glass.
b A ray of light is incident on a rectangular block of glass. What is the maximum angle of refraction in the glass?

Answer

a $n = \dfrac{\sin 90}{\sin c} = \dfrac{1}{\sin c} = \dfrac{1}{\sin 41.8°} = 1.50$

b the critical angle for the glass

> **Knowledge check 39**
>
> The outline of the practical procedure suggests that points drawn in the incident ray should be as far apart as possible. Why is this good practice?

Refinement

There is an alternative approach to measuring the critical angle. When the refracted ray is just seen emerging along the diameter, the angle of incidence could be increased by an extremely small amount so that total internal reflection takes place. The angle between the incident ray and this reflected ray is, within the limits of experimental error, equal to $2c$. This has the advantage that the totally internally reflected ray will be very bright, so it is particularly easy to draw the ray and measure $2c$.

> **Exam tip**
>
> You must be able to recall an accurate definition of critical angle. For example: the critical angle is the angle of incidence in glass when the angle of refraction in air is 90°.

Practical activity 14

Determine the focal length of a converging lens and verify experimentally the lens equation for real images

Background information

The distant object method is an inaccurate way of finding the focal length of a converging lens and inappropriate for A-level.

A better way is to use the lens equation: $\dfrac{1}{u} + \dfrac{1}{v} = \dfrac{1}{f}$, where u is the distance between the lens and the object, v is the distance between the lens and the real image on the screen and f is the focal length.

> **Exam tip**
>
> Make sure you know your definitions thoroughly. The focal length of a lens is the distance between its optical centre and the principal focus.

Practical activities

A lamphouse, a lens in a holder and a screen are arranged on an optical bench. If an optical bench is not available, a metre stick taped to the bench will serve almost as well. The object is taken as the mesh or cross wires at the front of the lamphouse.

Practical procedure

1. The lamphouse is placed at a distance from the lens greater than the approximate value of the focal length (Figure 49).
2. The screen is positioned close to, but on the opposite side of, the lens.
3. The screen is moved away from the lens until a sharp, inverted image of the cross wires image appears on the screen.
4. If no such image can be obtained, it is probable that the object is within the focal length. Increase the distance u and start again.
5. The distances u and v are measured using the metre stick.
6. The procedure is repeated for different values u and the results are recorded as shown in Table 20.

> **Knowledge check 40**
> The Practical procedure states that, if an image cannot be obtained, it is probable that the object is within the focal length. Explain this statement.

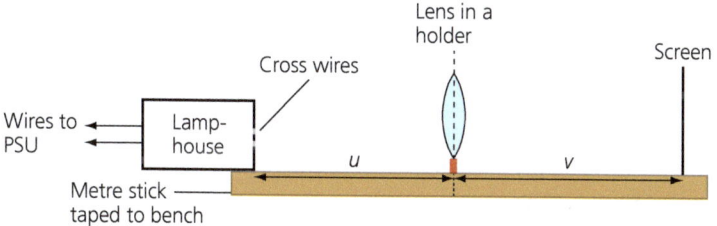

Figure 49 Experimental set-up to determine the focal length of a converging lens

Table 20 Experimental results

Object distance u/m	0.30	0.35	0.40	0.45	0.50	0.55
Image distance v/m	0.60	0.47	0.40	0.36	0.33	0.31
$\frac{1}{u}$/m^{-1}	3.33	2.86	2.50	2.22	2.00	1.82
$\frac{1}{v}$/m^{-1}	1.67	2.13	2.50	2.78	3.03	3.23

Analysis of the results

We can map the lens equation to the general equation of a straight line:

$$\frac{1}{f} = \frac{1}{u} + \frac{1}{v}$$

$$\frac{1}{v} = -1\left(\frac{1}{u}\right) + \frac{1}{f}$$

Compare this with $y = mx + c$.

A graph of $\frac{1}{v}$ (vertical axis) against $\frac{1}{u}$ (horizontal axis) will give a straight line of gradient -1 and an intercept on the vertical axis of $\frac{1}{f}$ (Figure 50). The graph intercepts the horizontal axis at the point where $\frac{1}{v} = 0$. Hence, the intercept on the horizontal axis is also $\frac{1}{f}$. The graph plotted should therefore be extended to cross

Content Guidance

both axes and the average intercept found. The reciprocal of this average intercept is taken as the focal length.

The graph also serves as verification of the lens equation.

Uncertainty in the experimental data

Although the metre stick may be calibrated in mm, the major cause of uncertainty in this experiment is the human eye. That is because there is a range of image distances (around 5 mm) over which the image on the screen is equally sharp. It is reasonable therefore to take the maximum uncertainty in the readings as 0.5 cm.

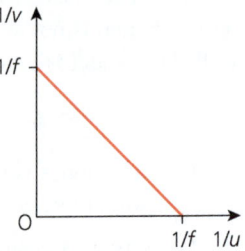

Figure 50 Graph to find the focal length of a converging lens

> **Worked example**
>
> **a** Assuming the maximum uncertainty in u and v is 0.5 cm, what is the maximum absolute uncertainty in the values of $\frac{1}{u}$ and $\frac{1}{v}$ in the results in Table 20?
>
> **b** What is the maximum % uncertainty in the quantity $(\frac{1}{u} + \frac{1}{v})$?
>
> **c** Hence, state the maximum absolute uncertainty in the value of f.
>
> **Answer**
>
> **a** Maximum % uncertainty in $u = \frac{0.5}{30} \times 100\%$
>
> $= 1.7\% =$ maximum % uncertainty in $\frac{1}{u}$
>
> Maximum absolute uncertainty in $\frac{1}{u} = 1.7\% \times 3.33 = 0.057\,\text{m}^{-1}$
>
> Maximum % uncertainty in $v = \frac{0.5}{31} \times 100\%$
>
> $= 1.7\% =$ maximum % uncertainty in $\frac{1}{v}$
>
> Maximum absolute uncertainty in $\frac{1}{v} = 1.7\% \times 3.23 = 0.055\,\text{m}^{-1}$
>
> **b** Maximum absolute uncertainty in $\frac{1}{u} + \frac{1}{v} = 0.057 + 0.055 = 0.11\,\text{m}^{-1}$
>
> **c** Maximum % uncertainty in $\frac{1}{f} = \frac{0.11}{5} \times 100\% = 2.2\%$
>
> Maximum absolute uncertainty in $f = 2.2\% \times 0.20\,\text{m} = 4.4\,\text{mm}$

Knowledge check 41

The graph of u (vertical axis) against v (horizontal axis) is a curve of negative gradient. The straight line $u = v$ intersects this curve at point P. In what way are the coordinates of point P related to the focal length f?

Practical activity 15

Verify that the magnification of a real image is equal to the ratio of the image distance to the object distance

Background information

The magnification M of a real image is *defined* as the ratio of the image height to the object height. In this experiment, M is shown to be also equal to the ratio of the image distance to the object distance. At the same time, we obtain a relationship between M and f and use it to measure the focal length of the lens.

66 CCEA AS/A2 Physics Unit 3

Practical activities

Practical procedure

1. The lamphouse is placed at a distance from the lens greater than the approximate value of the focal length (Figure 51).
2. The vertical diameter of the cross wires on the lamphouse is determined using a pair of dividers and a ruler.
3. The screen is positioned close to, but on the opposite side of, the lens.
4. The screen, which is covered with a sheet of graph paper having mm squares, is moved away from the lens until a sharp, inverted image of the cross wires image appears on the grid.
5. If no such image can be obtained, it is probable that the object is within the focal length. Increase the distance u and start again.
6. The distances u and v are measured using the metre stick.
7. For each value of u, the height of the image is measured on the graph paper grid on the screen.
8. The procedure is repeated for different values u and the results are recorded as shown in Table 21.

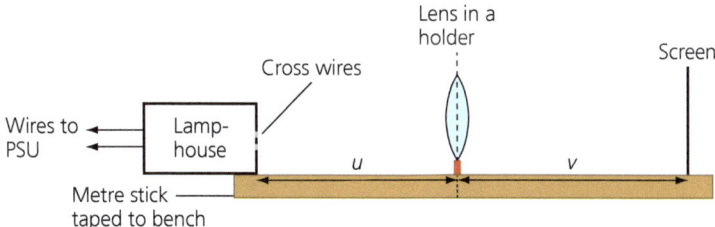

Figure 51 Experimental set-up

Analysis of the results

Height of object $h_o = 10\,\text{mm}$

Table 21 Typical experimental results

Object distance u/cm	30	35	40	45	50	55
Image distance v/cm	60	47	40	36	33	31
Ratio v/u	2.00	1.34	1.00	0.80	0.66	0.56
Height of image, h_i/mm	20	13	10	8	7	6
$M = h_i/h_o$	2.0	1.3	1.0	0.8	0.7	0.6

Table 21 demonstrates that, within the limits of experimental error, the magnification M is numerically equal to the ratio $\dfrac{v}{u}$.

> **Worked example**
>
> **a** Starting with the lens equation show that a graph of M against v is a straight line of intercept -1 on the vertical axis, intercept f on the horizontal axis and gradient $\dfrac{1}{v}$.
>
> **b** Plot the graph of M against v using the data in Table 21 and hence find the focal length of the lens.

Content Guidance

Answer

a From the lens equation we have: $\frac{1}{u} + \frac{1}{v} = \frac{1}{f}$

Multiplying both sides by v gives: $\frac{v}{u} + 1 = \frac{v}{f}$

But from the experiment, $\frac{v}{u} = M$ $\quad M + 1 = \frac{v}{f}$

Rearranging gives: $M = -1 + (\frac{1}{f})v$ [equation 1]

Compare with the straight-line equation: $y = c + mx$

So, the graph of M (vertical axis) against v (horizontal axis) gives a straight line of gradient $\frac{1}{f}$ and intercept -1.

On the horizontal axis $M = 0$. Substituting $M = 0$ in equation 1 gives:

$0 = -1 + (\frac{1}{f})v$

Multiplying by f and rearranging gives: $v = f$

Hence, the intercept on the horizontal axis is also equal to f.

We therefore plot this graph and determine f from the gradient ($f = \frac{1}{\text{gradient}}$) and the intercept on the *horizontal* axis. The mean of these two values is taken as the best value of f.

b

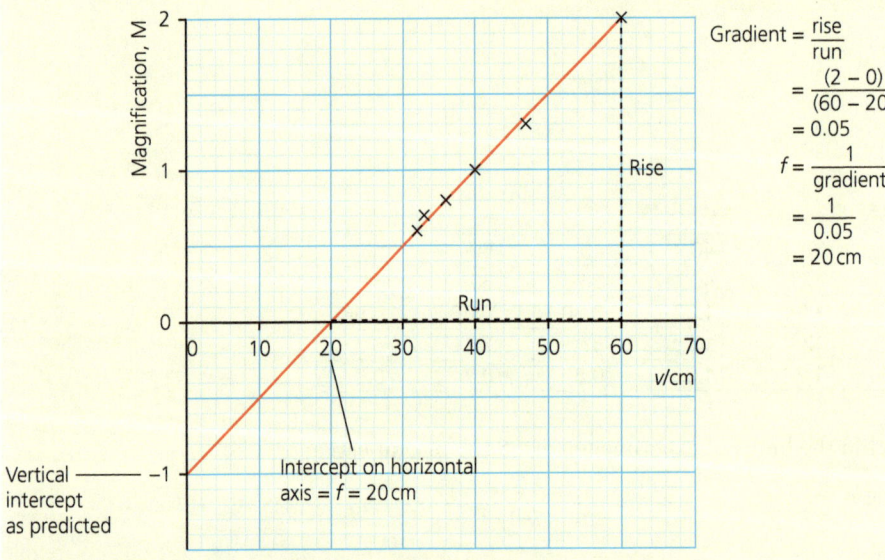

Figure 52 Graphical treatment of experimental results

Focal length = 20 cm

> **Exam tip**
>
> All graphs should use at least half the grid and have a scale which is easy to manage. Plot points accurately, in pencil, with each shown as a small cross or a dot within a circle. All straight lines should be drawn with a ruler.

> **Knowledge check 42**
>
> a State the independent, dependent and control variables in the experiment to find f by the magnification method.
>
> b The major uncertainty in the experiment is in the determination of v. Is this uncertainty caused by a systematic or random error? Explain your answer.
>
> c How might a group of students working together reduce the uncertainty?

Practical activity 16

Determine the speed of sound in air using a resonance tube

Background information

Sound waves of known frequency are produced using a signal generator and a loudspeaker (Figure 53). The sound waves are propagated down a tube and reflected at the closed end. Stationary waves are produced by the interference of the incident and reflected waves. The air is at rest at the closed end which is therefore a node. For resonance the open end must be an antinode. The distance between a node and an adjacent antinode is equal to $\frac{\lambda}{4}$.

The distance between the closed end of the tube and the open end is measured to determine the wavelength. Since the frequency of the incident waves is known, the speed can be found from the wave equation $v = f\lambda$.

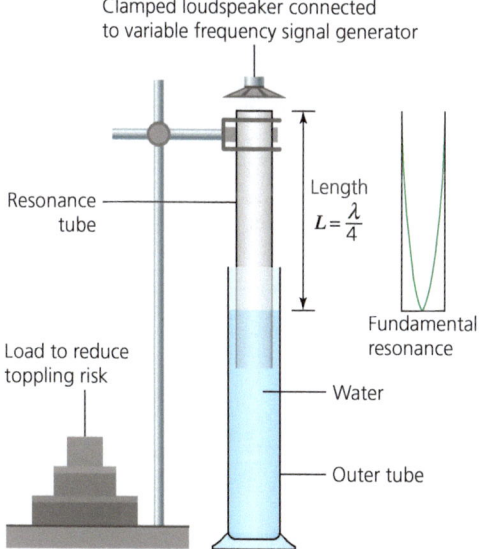

Figure 53 Experimental set-up

Practical procedure

1. The length of the air column L is set to 20 cm.
2. The frequency of the signal generator is then slowly increased from zero to a value f at which the sound from the resonance tube is loudest. This represents fundamental resonance for this air column.
3. The process is repeated for different lengths L from 20 cm to about 80 cm in steps of 10 cm.
4. The lengths L and the corresponding frequencies f are recorded in a table, similar to Table 22.

Table 22 Typical results

Length L/m	0.20	0.30	0.40	0.50	0.60	0.70	0.80
Frequency f/Hz	416	283	213	170	142	121	106
$\frac{1}{f}$ ms	2.4	3.5	4.7	5.9	7.1	8.2	9.4

> **Knowledge check 43**
> a State one way in which stationary waves are different from progressive waves.
> b What is the distance between consecutive nodes in a stationary wave?

> **Knowledge check 44**
> Why is it important to increase the frequency of the signal generator very slowly and to start at zero?

> **Exam tip**
> It is not enough to say that resonance is detected when the sound from the tube is loud (or even very loud). Examiners are looking to see if you know that at resonance the sound is at its loudest.

Content Guidance

Worked example

a What are the dependent and independent variables in this experiment?
b At any given length there is a series of resonance frequencies f, $3f$, $5f$ and so on. Why is this?
c Show that the graph of L against $\frac{1}{f}$ is a straight line of gradient $\frac{v}{4}$, where v is the speed of sound.
d Use the data in Table 22 to plot this graph and find the speed of sound.

Answer

a Independent: frequency of the sound f. Dependent: resonance length L
b These are resonance frequencies at fundamental, 3rd harmonic and 5th harmonic.
c Since $v = f\lambda$ and $\lambda = 4L$, we can write $v = 4fL$.

Rearranging gives: $L = \frac{v}{4} \times \frac{1}{f}$

Compare with the equation of a straight line $y = mx + c$.

So, a graph of L against $\frac{1}{f}$ should yield a straight line through the origin of gradient of $\frac{v}{4}$.

d
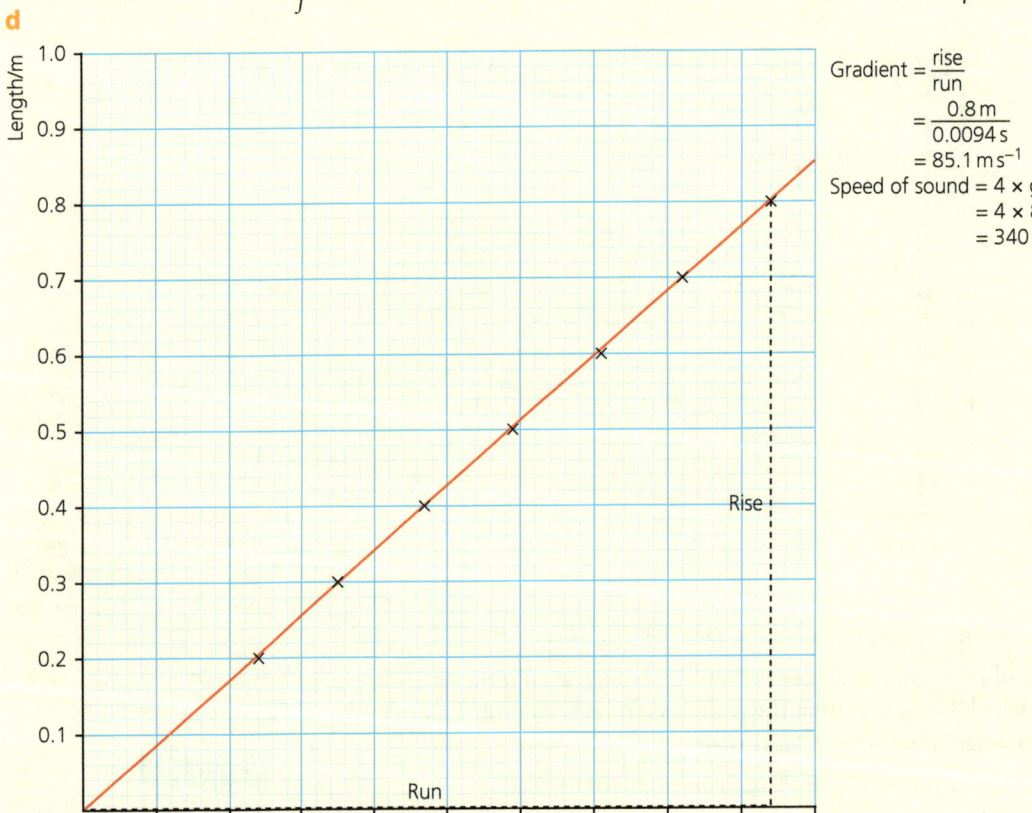

Figure 54 Graph to find the speed of sound

From the graph, the speed of sound = $340 \, \text{m s}^{-1}$.

Practical activities

Practical activity 17

Determine the wavelength of light using a double slit

Background information

The original experiment was carried out by Thomas Young in the nineteenth century using **monochromatic** light. This experiment is a modern equivalent using laser light which is both monochromatic and **coherent**.

The laser beam (from, for example, a white board pointer) is directed at a double slit, as shown in Figure 55. Interference fringes will be visible on a screen placed about 2 m away.

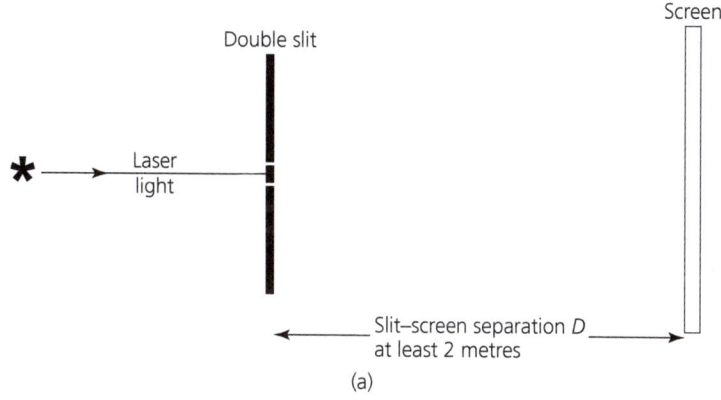

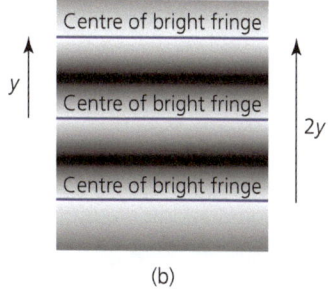

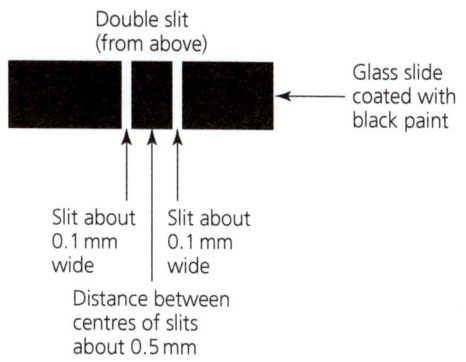

Figure 55 The double-slit experiment

> **Exam tip**
>
> Examiners are always looking for the precautions which students need to take to ensure a satisfactory experimental result. Make sure you know at least one precaution for every experiment.

Monochromatic Having a single wavelength.

Coherent A constant phase difference between the waves.

Practical techniques and data analysis 71

Content Guidance

Practical procedure

1. The distance D between the slits and the screen is measured with a tape.
2. The distance across as many fringes as possible is measured with a ruler and divided by the number of fringes in order to find the fringe separation y.
3. Typically, the manufacturer of the double slit will provide a data sheet giving the separation y. If not, the separation can be measured independently with a travelling microscope.
4. The experiment involves measuring the fringe separation y for various distances D, ranging from about 2 m to about 4 m.

> **Knowledge check 45**
>
> Suggest why it is a good idea to carry out the experiment in a darkened room.

Safety

The main hazard in this experiment relates to the use of laser light. Although the lasers used in schools have a low power (about 1 mW), they present a serious risk of eye injury if the user looks directly into the beam. Lasers must be switched off except when actually being used. There is also the risk of specular reflection of the laser light from shiny surfaces in the laboratory. This can cause eye damage without the person's knowledge. Shiny surfaces should be covered with dark paper. Finally, there is the problem of other people entering the laboratory on legitimate business, but unaware of the dangers of laser light. While lasers are being used there should be a notice on the entrance door requesting visitors to knock and remain outside until authorised to enter.

Analysis of results

The wavelength equation is given to you in your formula sheet. You do not need to know how it is derived. The wavelength λ is related to the fringe width y by the equation $D = \frac{a}{\lambda} \times y$. If we compare this equation with that for a straight line through the origin $y = mx$, we see that a graph of D against y is a straight line through (0, 0) with gradient $\frac{a}{\lambda}$. The wavelength is therefore equal to $\frac{a}{\text{gradient}}$.

> **Worked example**
>
> A student carried out the experiment outlined above to determine the wavelength of a beam of monochromatic light using a double slit of width 0.1 mm. The student obtained the results in Table 23.
>
> **Table 23** Typical results
>
> | Distance d/m | 2.0 | 2.4 | 2.8 | 3.2 | 3.6 | 4.0 |
> |---|---|---|---|---|---|---|
> | Number of fringes | 15 | 14 | 12 | 10 | 10 | 8 |
> | Separation/mm | 207 | 231 | 232 | 221 | 248 | 221 |
> | Fringe width y/mm | 14 | 17 | 19 | 22 | 25 | 28 |
>
> Plot a suitable straight-line graph and use it to find the wavelength of the light. Give your answer in nanometres.

Practical activities

Answer

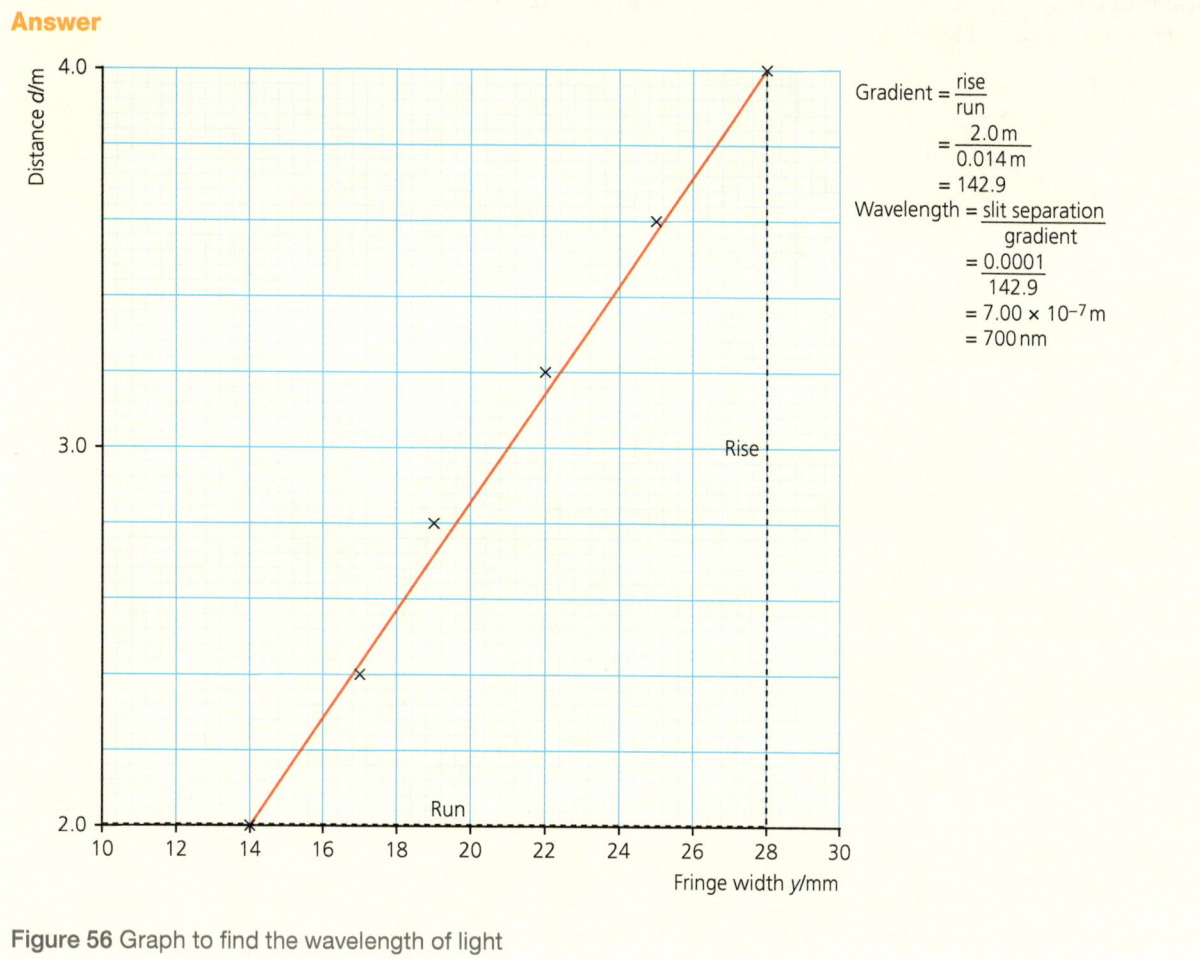

Figure 56 Graph to find the wavelength of light

Practical activity 18

Determine the wavelength of light using a diffraction grating

Background information

A grating is an opaque glass slide on which there are many machine-ruled, parallel score lines, each the same distance apart. This is called a grating element and is given the symbol d. It is therefore like a Young's fringes double slit, but there are perhaps thousands of lines on a single grating with a separation of around 0.5 micrometre, which is comparable to the wavelength of light.

When light passes through a grating, the main effect taking place is diffraction. The light spreads as it passes through each slit, as shown in Figure 57. These diffracted

Exam tip

Calculations on the wavelength of visible light are common in AS examinations. Always check that your answers are reasonable. The wavelength of visible light lies between 400 nm (violet) and 700 nm (red).

beams interfere with each other and the result is a series of fringes which can be observed on a screen (Figure 58).

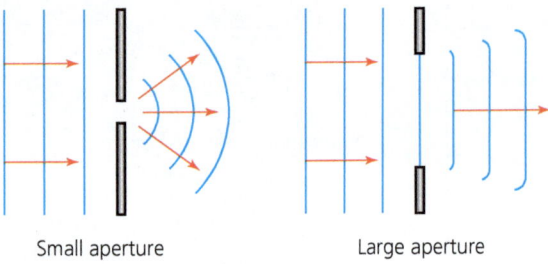

Small aperture   Large aperture

Figure 57 Diffraction at a single slit

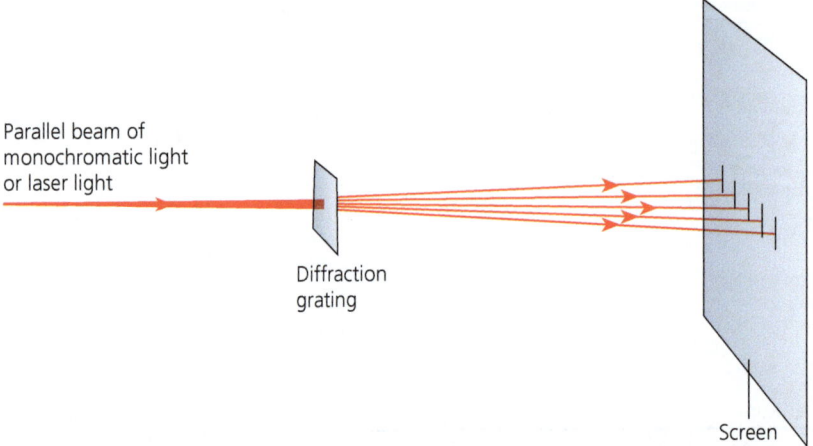

Figure 58 Diffraction of monochromatic light by a grating produces fringes

The fringes are not equally spaced and they are not of equal intensity. The fringe caused by light passing through the grating is called the zero-order or $n = 0$ fringe. The fringe on either side of it is called the first order or $n = 1$ fringe, and so on.

The angle between the zero-order beam and any other beam is called the angle of diffraction θ. The mathematical relationship between the angle of diffraction θ and the grating element d is:

$d \sin \theta = n\lambda$

Finding the wavelength of light therefore requires us to measure the value of θ for a given value of n, since d is supplied by the grating manufacturer. It is easiest to use the first-order fringes because they are so bright.

Practical procedure

1. A commercial diffraction grating of known element is mounted in a suitable holder and placed between a suitable light source and a screen (Figure 59).

Practical activities

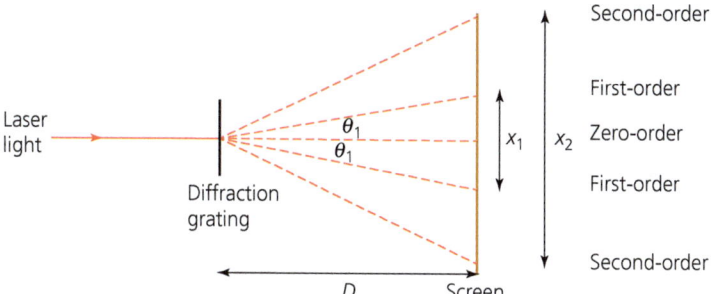

Figure 59 Diffraction at a grating

2   The distance D between the grating and the screen is measured with a measuring tape.
3   Monochromatic light, whose wavelength λ is to be measured, is directed normally at the grating.
4   The distance x_1 between the first-order maxima is measured with a ruler, calibrated in mm.
5   The angle θ_1 for the first order is calculated using $\theta_1 = \tan^{-1}(\tfrac{1}{2}x_1/D)$.
6   This process is repeated using the same light source, but with gratings of different grating element, d.
7   Since $d \sin \theta = n\lambda$, then $d \sin \theta_1 = 1 \times \lambda$.

Analysis of results

Since $d \sin \theta_1 = \lambda$, a graph of d against $(\sin \theta_1)^{-1}$ will be a straight line through the origin of gradient equal to the wavelength of the light (Figure 60).

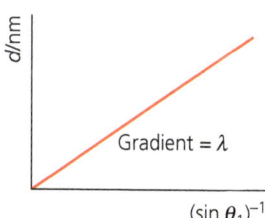

Figure 60 Graphical treatment of results of diffraction experiment

Worked example

a   A manufacturer advises that the supplied diffraction grating has 400 lines per mm. Calculate the size of the grating element.
b   A student measures the angle of diffraction in the third order to be 37°. Calculate the wavelength of the light being used.
c   The same grating is used with light of wavelength 680 nm. What is the angle of diffraction in the second order for this light?

Answer

a $d = \dfrac{1}{N} = \dfrac{1}{400} = 2.5 \times 10^{-3}\,\text{mm}$

b $\lambda = \dfrac{d \times \sin \theta}{3} = \dfrac{2.5 \times 10^{-3} \times \sin 37}{3} = 5.02 \times 10^{-4}\,\text{mm} = 502\,\text{nm}$

c $\theta = \sin^{-1} \dfrac{n\lambda}{d} = \sin^{-1} \dfrac{2 \times 680 \times 10^{-9}}{2.5 \times 10^{-6}} = 33.0°$

Knowledge check 46

What happens to the width of the maxima and their brightness when the grating element decreases?

Exam tip

The equation $d = \dfrac{1}{N}$, used to find the width of the grating element, is not given in your Data and Formulae sheet. But it is so straightforward and so useful that it is worthwhile remembering.

Practical techniques and data analysis

Content Guidance

Practical activity 19
Determine the Young modulus for the material of a metal wire

Background information
A tensile stress σ applied to a material produces a strain ε. Stress is defined as the tensile force per unit area. Strain is defined as the extension divided by the original length of the specimen wire. Provided the stress is not too large, the strain is directly proportional to the stress.

Within the limit of proportionality, the ratio $\dfrac{\sigma}{\varepsilon}$ is defined as the Young modulus E. Measuring the Young modulus will therefore involve measuring stress and strain for a wire under tension. The apparatus required to find the Young modulus of copper in the form of a long wire is shown in Figure 61.

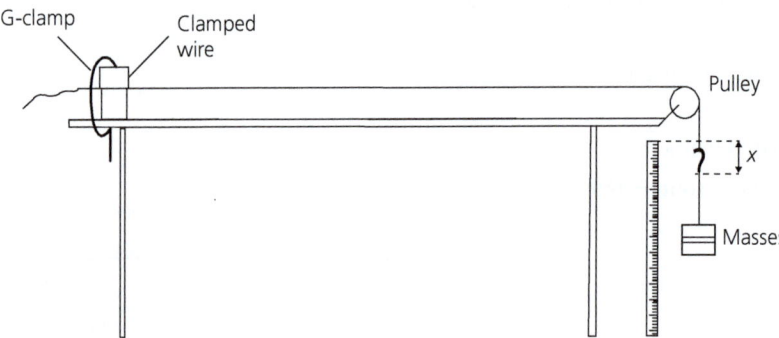

Figure 61 Apparatus to find the Young modulus

Practical procedure
1. The original length of wire to be stretched is measured with a tape.
2. The diameter of the wire at six different points along its length is found with a micrometer and the mean value calculated.
3. Using $A = \dfrac{\pi d^2}{4}$, the mean cross-section area is calculated.
4. A metre ruler with mm gradations is clamped vertically with the zero opposite the end of the unstretched, but straight and kink-free, wire.
5. Loads from 100 g (approx. 1 N) up to 800 g in steps of 100 g are placed on the mass carrier and, for each, the extension is measured using the vertical ruler.
6. The results are recorded as shown in Table 24.

Safety
The major hazard in this experiment is the potential for the load and carrier to become detached from the wire. This can have two consequences. First, the wire can whip back with the risk of serious eye injury to students and staff. The other consequence is that a load, even as small as 1 kg, can cause harm if it falls on someone's toes.

To mitigate the risk of eye injury, everyone involved in this practical activity must wear safety glasses/goggles. To prevent potential harm from a falling mass, a soft cushion or schoolbag should be placed on the floor under the load.

Practical activities

Worked example

The results of the Young modulus investigation are shown in Table 24.

Length of unstretched wire = 2.00 m

Diameter/mm = 0.10, 0.10, 0.11, 0.10, 0.10, 0.09

Mean csa = 7.854×10^{-9} m^2

Table 24 Young modulus experimental data

Load/N	1.0	2.0	3.0	4.0	5.0	6.0	7.0	8.0
Extension/mm	2	4	6	8	10	12	14	16
Stress σ/MPa	127	254	381	508	635	762	889	1016
Strain ε ($\times 10^{-3}$)	1.0	2.0	3.0	4.0	5.0	6.0	7.0	8.0

a Show that the gradient of a graph of stress against strain for the stretched copper wire is equal to the Young modulus E.

b Plot the graph of stress against strain and use it to find the value of E.

Suppose a 1.000 m length of the copper wire used in this investigation (diameter 0.10 mm) is welded to another wire of the same dimensions but having twice the Young modulus to form a composite wire of length 2.000 m. When it is then subjected to a tensile stress, the length of the composite wire increases to 2.006 m.

c Calculate the tensile force in each wire.

Answer

a Since $E = \dfrac{\sigma}{\varepsilon}$, rearranging gives $\sigma = E\varepsilon$.

Compare this with the straight-line equation $y = mx$.

So, a graph of stress σ against strain ε will give a straight line through the origin of gradient equal to the Young modulus E.

b Figure 62 shows that $E = 127$ GPa.

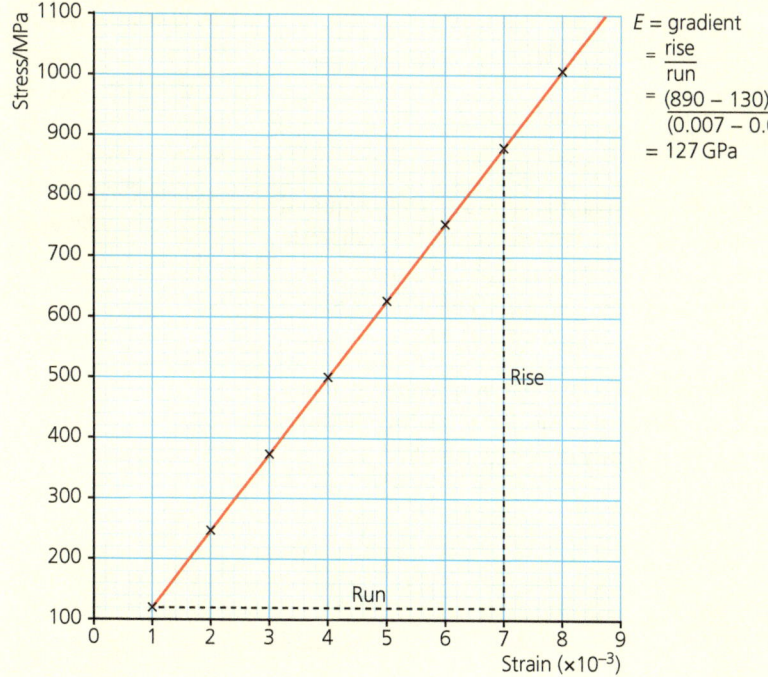

E = gradient
= $\dfrac{\text{rise}}{\text{run}}$
= $\dfrac{(890 - 130)\,\text{MPa}}{(0.007 - 0.001)}$
= 127 GPa

Figure 62 Graph to find the Young modulus

Content Guidance

c Since the wires have exactly the same dimensions, the stress in each is the same. So the extension in each is inversely proportional to the value of E.

So, copper has an extension of 4 mm and the other wire has an extension of 2 mm.

The strain in copper is $\dfrac{\text{extension}}{\text{original length}} = \dfrac{4}{1000} = 0.004$.

The strain in the other wire is $\dfrac{\text{extension}}{\text{original length}} = \dfrac{2}{1000} = 0.002$.

The stress is the product of the Young modulus and the strain.

Stress in copper $= 0.004 \times 127 \times 10^9 = 508$ MPa.

Stress in the other wire $= 0.002 \times 2 \times 127 \times 10^9 = 508$ MPa.

Force in copper = force in the other wire = stress × csa
$$= 508 \times 10^9 \times 7.854 \times 10^{-9} = 3.99 \text{ kN}$$

Important observations

At higher stress, the graph ceases to be a straight line. This is because the wire ceases to be elastic – much like the graph of force against extension curves in a Hooke's law investigation.

In this experiment, a millimetre scale was chosen to measure the extension. This is only possible when using soft metals, such as copper, which have a particularly low value of E. Other metals, such as hardened steel, have values of E which are more than twice that of copper. For such materials, the physicist must use a different technique to measure the extension. Usually this involves the use of a Vernier scale which can measure the extension to within 0.1 mm.

Practical activity 20

Perform and describe an electrical method for determining specific heat capacity (of a liquid)

Background information

The specific heat capacity (SHC) of a material is the quantity of heat energy required to raise the temperature of 1 kg of that material by 1 °C. This definition leads directly to the equation $Q = mC\Delta T$, where Q = quantity of heat supplied, m = mass of material, C = specific heat capacity and ΔT = rise in temperature. The unit for SHC is J kg^{-1} K^{-1} (or J kg^{-1} °C^{-1}).

Measurement of SHC requires us to supply a measured quantity of heat energy to a known mass of material and measure its temperature rise. Electrical heating methods are preferred because it is easy to determine the quantity of energy supplied.

> **Exam tip**
> Always be very careful when using different non-standard units in mathematical questions. For example, GPa, MPa and kPa should all be converted to Pa before any arithmetic is carried out.

> **Knowledge check 47**
> Concrete is very strong in compression and weak in tension. Why then are steel rods placed in the concrete beams used in the construction of bridges?

Practical activities

Practical procedure

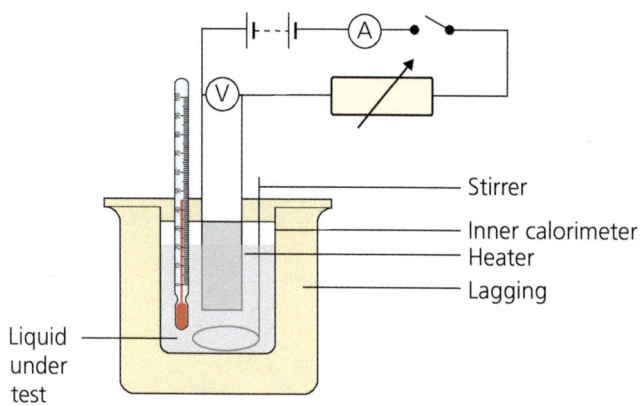

Figure 63 Apparatus to find the specific heat capacity of a liquid

1. Weigh a clean, dry, empty copper calorimeter on a digital balance.
2. Half fill the calorimeter with the liquid under test and re-weigh.
3. Subtract the readings to find the mass of the liquid.
4. Place the calorimeter in a beaker which is well insulated on the inside.
5. Insert a thermometer, electrical heater and stirrer in the holes in the lid and place it on top of the beaker.
6. Connect the ammeter, voltmeter, PSU, rheostat and switch, as shown in Figure 63.
7. Switch on the PSU and set the voltage to 12 V using the rheostat.
8. Record the initial temperature of the liquid, the voltage and the current, and start a stopwatch.
9. Stir the liquid regularly throughout the experiment.
10. After 10 minutes stop the stopwatch and switch off the PSU.
11. Allow the experiment to continue and record the maximum temperature of the liquid.

> **Exam tip**
> Stir the liquid to ensure the liquid and the calorimeter are at the same temperature and the thermometer is accurately measuring the temperature of both.

> **Exam tip**
> When heating has stopped, observe the thermometer and take the highest reading. This is because it may take a short while for the heat to transfer from the immersion heater to the liquid.

Worked example

A student records the results of her experiment in columnar form as shown below.

Mass of empty calorimeter, in kg:	0.20
Mass of calorimeter plus liquid, in kg:	0.65
Mass of liquid m, in kg:	0.45
Current in heater, in A:	5.0
Voltage across heater, in V:	12.0
Power of heater P, in W:	60
Time heater on t, in s:	300
Heat supplied $H = P \times t$, in J:	18 000
Initial temperature of liquid, in °C:	14.5

> **Knowledge check 48**
> What is the purpose of the rheostat in this experiment?

Content Guidance

Maximum temperature of liquid, in °C:	23.5
Rise in temperature of liquid ΔT, in °C:	9.0
SHC of copper (in calorimeter), in J kg^{-1} °C^{-1}:	385

Use these results to calculate:
a the heat gained by the calorimeter
b the heat supplied to the liquid
c the specific heat capacity of the liquid

Some students claim that ignoring the heat lost to the calorimeter itself makes little difference to the calculated value for C.

d State whether or not you agree, justifying your answer with a suitable calculation.

Answer
a Heat gained by calorimeter $= mC\Delta T = 0.20 \times 385 \times 9 = 693$ J
b Heat supplied to liquid $Q = H - 693 = 18\,000 - 693 = 17\,307$ J
c SHC of liquid $= Q/(m\,\Delta T) = \dfrac{17\,307}{0.45 \times 9} = 4273$ J kg^{-1} °C^{-1}
d The heat lost to the calorimeter itself in the calculation above (693 J) is very much less than that supplied to the liquid, so it is likely that ignoring it will make little difference. In that case, $C = \dfrac{18\,000}{0.45 \times 9} = 4444$ J kg^{-1} °C^{-1} (as opposed to 4273 J kg^{-1} °C^{-1}).

Refinement
The SHC found in this experiment is invariably *larger* than the generally accepted value. This is because heat is *always* lost from the warm liquid and the calorimeter to the surroundings, even when the insulation is very good. Consequently, the temperature rise ΔT is less than would be expected. Since ΔT appears in the denominator, the calculated value of C is larger than the true value.

One way to reduce this error is to chill the liquid in a refrigerator to a temperature around 5 °C below room temperature before the experiment begins and to heat it only to about 5 °C above room temperature during the experiment. By doing so the heat lost to the environment when the liquid is above room temperature should cancel out the heat gained from the environment when the temperature is below room temperature. This should result in a calculated value of C closer to that which is generally accepted.

Practical activity 21
Investigate experimentally the motion of the simple pendulum and the loaded spiral spring

Background information: simple pendulum
Theory shows that the oscillations of a simple pendulum are approximately simple harmonic, provided the amplitude is small, and that the period T depends on the length l according to the equation:

$$T = 2\pi \sqrt{\dfrac{l}{g}} \quad \text{[equation 1]}$$

Practical activities

(Equation 1 is not required recall. It is given in the Data and Formulae sheet in your exam.)

The pendulum is best suspended by threading the supporting string through a split cork which is held tightly by a clamp attached to a retort stand, as shown in Figure 64.

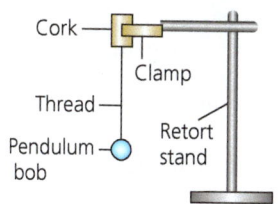

Figure 64 Simple pendulum set-up

Practical procedure

1. There are several necessary precautions when timing the pendulum:
   - Start timing only after the pendulum has completed a few oscillations and is at one extremum in its motion. This ensures that the measured time is not affected by transients at the start of the motion.
   - Avoid counting errors by saying 'zero' when starting the stopwatch.
   - Ensure that the measured time on the stopwatch is never less than about 20 s. Otherwise the % error in starting and stopping the stopwatch is excessively large.
   - These precautions apply when timing any *mechanical* oscillations. They are therefore equally valid when timing the oscillation of a loaded spiral spring.

2. The time for the pendulum to complete 20 oscillations is measured three times for lengths ranging from 30 cm to 100 cm in steps of 10 cm. This is necessary to minimise uncertainty in the period.

3. From these measurements, the period T for each length is determined, as shown in Table 25.

Table 25 Results of pendulum experiment

l/m	0.30	0.40	0.50	0.60	0.70	0.80	0.90	1.00
T/s	1.10	1.27	1.42	1.55	1.68	1.79	1.90	2.01
T^2/s^2	1.2							

Worked example

a Complete Table 25, entering the numbers for T^2 to 1 dp.
b Explain why equation 1 is only valid for small angles.
c What straight-line graph should be plotted to verify equation 1? Justify your answer.
d Plot this graph and use it to determine the acceleration due to gravity g.
e Explain why the motion is only approximately simple harmonic, even when the amplitude is small.

Answer

a

l/m	0.30	0.40	0.50	0.60	0.70	0.80	0.90	1.00
T/s	1.10	1.27	1.42	1.55	1.68	1.79	1.90	2.011
T^2/s^2	1.2	1.6	2.0	2.4	2.8	3.2	3.6	4.0

b The restoring force on the pendulum bob is $mg\sin\theta$.
For simple harmonic motion (SHM) to occur, the restoring force must be equal to $mg\theta$ where θ is in radians.
However, $\sin\theta$ is only approximately equal to θ when θ is small.

Exam tip

In calculations you sometimes have to use the small-angle approximations $\theta = \sin\theta \approx \tan\theta$. But remember that this is only true when θ is measured in radians.

Content Guidance

c From equation 1: $T = 2\pi\sqrt{\dfrac{l}{g}}$

Squaring: $T^2 = 4\pi^2\left(\dfrac{l}{g}\right)$

Expanding: $T^2 = \dfrac{4\pi^2}{g} \times l$

Comparing with $y = mx + c$, the graph of T^2 against l is a straight line through the origin with gradient $\dfrac{4\pi^2}{g}$ (Figure 65).

d
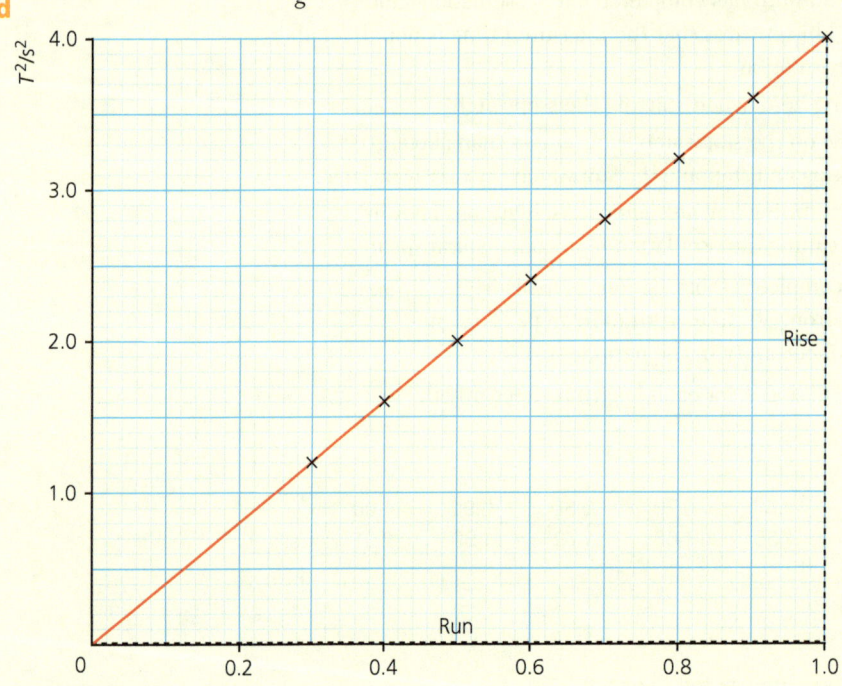

Figure 65 Simple pendulum graph to find g

$\text{gradient} = \dfrac{\text{rise}}{\text{run}} = \dfrac{4.0}{1.0}$
$= 4\,\text{s}^2\,\text{m}^{-1}$
$= \dfrac{4\pi^2}{g}$

$g = \dfrac{4\pi^2}{\text{gradient}} = \dfrac{4\pi^2}{4} = 9.97\,\text{m}\,\text{s}^{-2}$

e The amplitude of a simple harmonic motion does not change with time. But every simple pendulum eventually comes to rest because of friction. Its motion is therefore an example of a *damped* SHM. But it is isochronous, that is, its period remains the same, even as its amplitude decreases.

Background information: loaded spiral spring

Theory shows that the vertical oscillations of a loaded spiral spring are approximately simple harmonic and that the period T depends on the attached mass m and the spring constant k, according to the equation:

$T = 2\pi\sqrt{\dfrac{m}{k}}$ [equation 2]

> **Knowledge check 49**
>
> On the Moon the acceleration of free fall is approximately $1.6\,\text{m}\,\text{s}^{-2}$. What is the frequency of a 25 cm simple pendulum on the Moon?

> **Knowledge check 50**
>
> Why can we not use the equations of motion to determine the speed of a pendulum bob at the lowest point of its motion?

Practical activities

(Equation 2 is not required recall. It is given in the Data and Formulae sheet in your exam.) Equation 2 is only valid if the mass of the spring itself is much less than that of the attached mass m and if at all points in the motion the spring obeys Hooke's law.

The experiment to verify equation 2 works well with 2 cm 'expendable' springs. They are called 'expendable' because they are relatively inexpensive to replace. The spring is best suspended using two small wooden blocks which are held tightly by a clamp attached to a retort stand, as shown in Figure 66. An optical pin attached with Blu Tack ® to a clamped vertical ruler helps the student to see when the oscillating masses are at the centre of their motion.

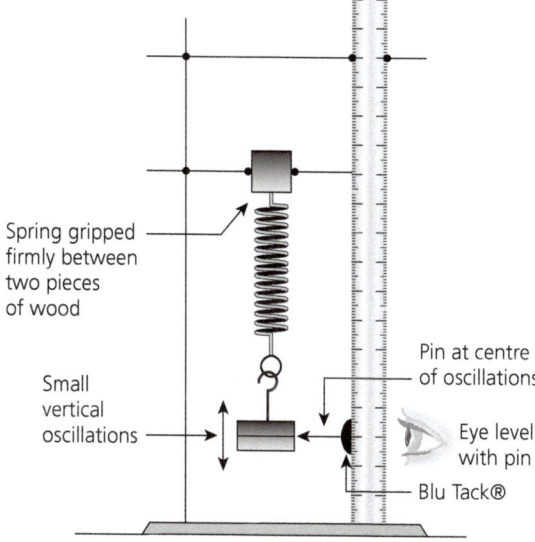

Figure 66 Oscillations in a loaded helical spring

Practical procedure

1 The time for the spring to complete 20 oscillations is measured three times for masses ranging from 200 g to 500 g in steps of 50 g. This is necessary to minimise uncertainty in the period. (Below 200 g the timing is difficult because the oscillation frequency is too high.)
2 From these measurements, the period T for each mass is determined, and the results entered in a pre-prepared table. See the Worked example, part c.

> **Exam tip**
> Always take sufficient repeats to be confident that your data are reliable. But remember you have a limited amount of time at each station in the exam. Too many repeats are as bad as too few.

Worked example

a State three safety precautions that should be taken when carrying out this experiment.
b State the dependent, independent and one control variable when conducting this experiment.
c Draw a suitable table in which data from this experiment might be recorded (no numerical data need be entered into the table).
d Sketch the graph you would expect to obtain if you plotted T against m.
e What straight-line graph might be plotted to verify equation 2?
f How might the spring constant be obtained from this straight-line graph? Justify your answer.

Practical techniques and data analysis 83

Content Guidance

Answer

a Wear safety goggles.

Place a shock pad on the retort stand below the oscillating masses.

Use a G-clamp to fix the retort stand to the bench to prevent it toppling over.

b Dependent: period; independent: mass attached; control: spring constant

c

m/g							
T_{20}/s							
T_{20}/s							
T_{20}/s							
Mean T/s							
T^2/s^2							

d

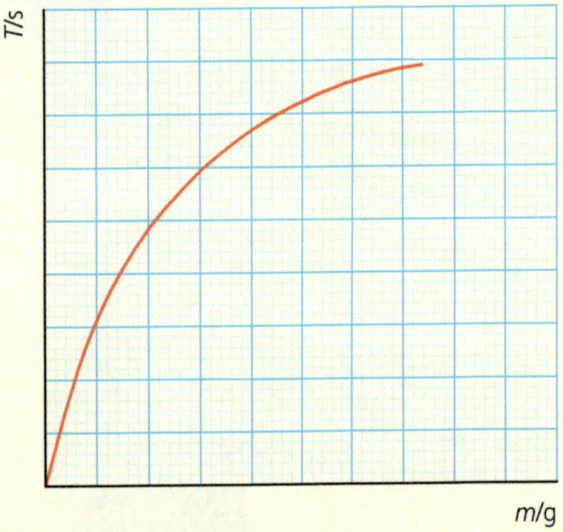

Figure 67 Graph of period against mass for an oscillating helical spring

e Plot T^2/s^2 against m/kg.

f From equation 2: $T = 2\pi\sqrt{\dfrac{m}{k}}$

Squaring: $T^2 = 4\pi^2\left(\dfrac{m}{k}\right)$

Expanding: $T^2 = \dfrac{4\pi^2}{k} \times m$

Comparing with $y = mx + c$, the graph of T^2 against m is a straight line through the origin with gradient $\dfrac{4\pi^2}{k}$.

so, k is $\dfrac{4\pi^2}{\text{gradient}}$

> **Knowledge check 51**
>
> Explain why the strain energy in the spring is a maximum when the masses are at the lowest and at the highest points in their motion.

Practical activity 22

Describe experiments to demonstrate the discharge and charge of a capacitor and measure the time constant

This series of experiments is to determine the voltage–time and current–time characteristic curves for (a) a discharging capacitor and (b) a charging capacitor and use them to find the time constant and the capacitance of the capacitor.

Practical activities

Background information

Discharging

The potential difference (p.d.) V across a discharging capacitor and the current I through it decrease exponentially with time t according to the equations:

$$V = V_0 e^{-t/RC}$$

where V_0 is the p.d. when $t = 0$ and

$$I = I_0 e^{-t/RC}$$

where I_0 is the current when $t = 0$ and $I_0 = V_0/R$.

The product RC is called the time constant τ. This is the time for the p.d. to fall to $\frac{1}{e}$ of its initial value, i.e. $0.368 \times V_0$.

The graphs of V against t and I against t are exponential decay curves. We map these to straight-line graphs by rearranging $\ln V$ into the form $y = mx + c$. Taking natural logs gives:

$$\ln V = \ln V_0 - \frac{1}{RC} \times t$$

and similarly:

$$\ln I = \ln I_0 - \frac{1}{RC} \times t$$

Compare with the general equation of a straight line, $y = c + mx$. If we plot a graph of $\ln V$ (or $\ln I$) on the y-axis against t on the x-axis, the gradient will be $-\frac{1}{RC}$ (or $-\frac{1}{\tau}$) and the intercept on the y-axis will be equal to $\ln V_0$ (or $\ln I_0$).

> **Knowledge check 52**
>
> For discharging capacitors, the voltage falls by a factor of $\frac{1}{e}$ in every time constant. By what percentage does the voltage across a discharging capacitor fall after 1, 2 and 3 time constants?

Charging

For a capacitor being charged by a battery of e.m.f. E through a resistor R, the corresponding equations are:

$$V = E(1 - e^{-t/RC})$$

and

$$I = I_0 e^{-t/RC}$$

where I_0 is the current when $t = 0$ and $I_0 = \frac{E}{R}$.

> **Knowledge check 53**
>
> When charging, the voltage rises to $(1 - e^{-n}) \times 100\%$ of the battery e.m.f. after n time constants. To what % of the battery e.m.f. does the voltage rise after 1, 2 and 3 time constants?

Practical procedure

The experimental arrangement to demonstrate how the voltage across a capacitor varies during charging and discharging is shown in Figure 68.

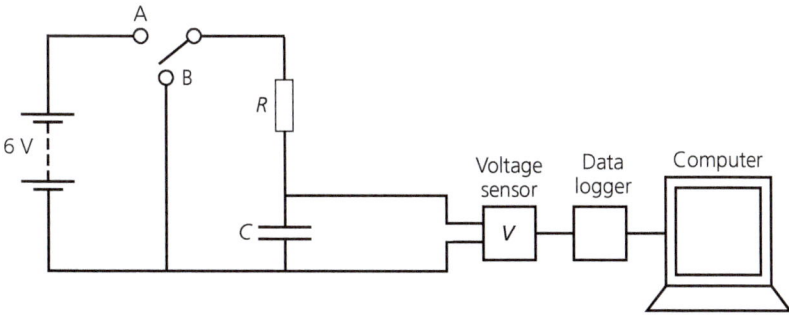

Figure 68 Circuit to investigate capacitors charging and discharging

Content Guidance

1. The capacitor is charged through the resistor by connecting the switch to contact A.
2. When the switch is later connected to contact B, the charged capacitor discharges through resistor R.
3. At all times the voltage across the capacitor is monitored and recorded by the datalogger and, later, it can be displayed as a voltage–time graph on the computer monitor.
4. To obtain current–time characteristics, a current sensor must be placed in series with the resistor and then connected to the datalogger and computer.
5. The graphs shown on the computer monitor might appear as sketched in Figure 69.

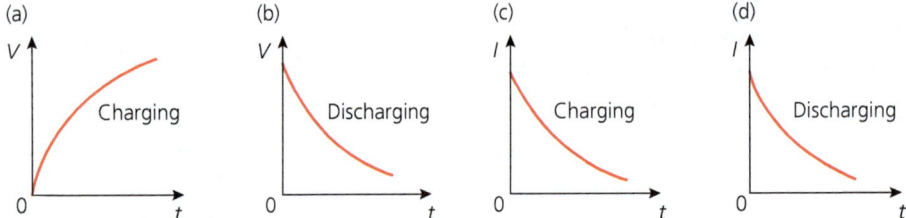

Figure 69 Capacitor charging and discharging graphs

Safety

- If an electrolytic capacitor is being used, one end of it will be marked + and the other end marked −. This polarity must be observed.
- The capacitors must be connected to a battery or a smoothed and regulated DC supply.
- Even though the voltages used are low, care should be taken to avoid short circuits.
- Capacitors can be dangerous because they can be rapidly discharged so care is needed.

The graphs in Figure 70 illustrate the relationship between the voltage and time for a discharging capacitor and another charging from 0 V by a battery of e.m.f. 10 V.

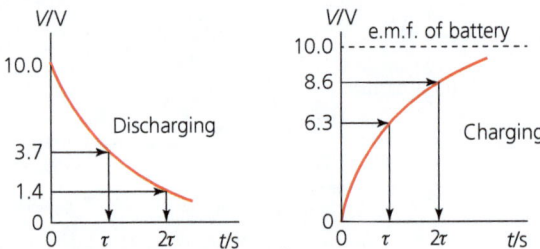

Figure 70 Finding the time constant from voltage–time graphs

Practical activities

Worked example

A capacitor of unknown value is discharged through a 330 kΩ resistor. Some of the voltage readings (V) from the datalogger are shown in Table 26.

Table 26 Capacitor discharge data

t/s	0.0	5.0	10.0	15.0	20.0	25.0	30.0	35.0	40.0
V/V	6.00	2.71	1.22	0.55	0.25	0.11	0.05	0.022	0.01
ln(V/V)									

a Complete the table by calculating the values of ln(V/V).
b Plot a graph of ln(V/V) against t/s and use it to determine a value for the time constant τ.
c Use the measured value of resistance to calculate the capacitance of the capacitor.

Answer

a Taking natural logs of the results in Table 26 produces:

t/s	0.0	5.0	10.0	15.0	20.0	25.0	30.0	35.0	40.0
ln(V/V)	1.79	1.00	0.20	−0.60	−1.4	−2.2	−3.0	−3.8	−4.6

b The graph and calculation of the time constant are shown in Figure 71.

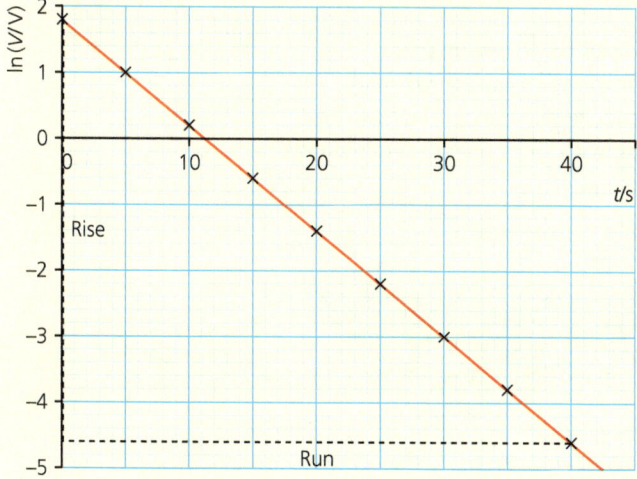

$$\text{Gradient} = \frac{\text{rise}}{\text{run}}$$
$$= \frac{-6.4}{40}$$
$$= -0.16$$
$$\text{Time constant} = \frac{-1}{\text{gradient}}$$
$$= \frac{-1}{-0.16}$$
$$= 6.25\,\text{s}$$

Figure 71 Linear graph of capacitor discharge

c Taking R = 330 kΩ and using $\tau = RC$ we get:

$$C = \frac{6.25}{330 \times 10^3} = 1.89 \times 10^{-5}\,\text{F} = 19\,\mu\text{F}$$

Exam tip

CCEA has never required candidates to use logarithmic graph paper in any of its physics examinations, but you are expected to be able to plot log graphs on ordinary graph paper.

Content Guidance

Practical activity 23

Describe how the cathode ray oscilloscope (CRO) can be used to determine the voltage and frequency

Background information

Sinusoidal electrical signals of different frequency and amplitude can be generated by a signal generator or oscillator. Such signals can be fed directly to the input terminals of a CRO, as shown in Figure 72.

Following adjustment of the time base (TB) control and sensitivity (gain) control, a visual representation of the signal can be seen on the screen of the CRO. Measurements taken directly from the CRO screen can be used to determine the frequency and amplitude of the input signal.

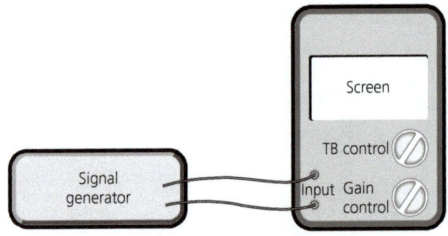

Figure 72 Experimental set-up

Be wary of talking about the distance between the peaks of the waves as the wavelength of the signal. It is not. Adjusting the TB control will adjust the display and hence the distance between the peaks, but the input signal has not changed! The distance between the peaks must be read in conjunction with the TB setting to obtain the period (and hence the frequency) of the signal.

Tables 27 and 28 show the purposes of the time base and gain controls.

Table 27 Adjusting the time base and gain controls

Input	Time base off	Time base on
DC (e.g. from a battery)	bright spot on screen	horizontal straight line
AC (e.g. from an oscillator)	vertical straight line	sinusoidal curve

Table 28 Changing the vertical height and peak separation

	To change the vertical height of the display	To change the separation of the peaks
AC signal	adjust the gain (or sensitivity) control	adjust the TB control

The key skill to be learned with a CRO is how to use the information provided by the TB and sensitivity controls to determine the frequency and amplitude of an AC signal.

The CRO is a particularly useful instrument for measuring voltage because:
- it has a nearly infinite resistance, so it draws very little current from the circuit under investigation
- it can be used for both AC and DC
- it has an almost instantaneous response

Practical activities

Worked example

Figure 73 shows two patterns seen on a CRO screen and their corresponding time base and gain settings. Use the information to calculate the frequency and amplitude of each signal.

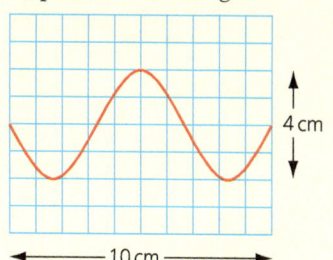
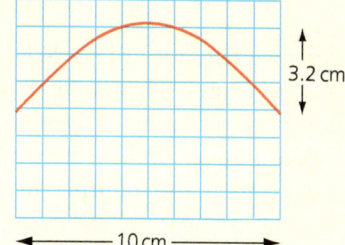

Figure 73 CRO patterns

Time base setting: $20\,\mu s\,cm^{-1}$
Gain setting: $5\,V\,cm^{-1}$

Time base setting: $100\,\mu s\,cm^{-1}$
Gain setting: $10\,V\,cm^{-1}$

Answer

Signal parameters:

Period $T = 6.7\,cm \times 20\,\mu s\,cm^{-1}$
$= 134\,\mu s = 1.34 \times 10^{-4}\,s$

Frequency $= \dfrac{1}{T} = \dfrac{1}{1.34 \times 10^{-4}}$
$= 7.5\,kHz$

Amplitude $= \tfrac{1}{2} \times 4\,cm \times 5\,V\,cm^{-1}$
$= 10\,V$

Signal parameters:

Period $T = 2 \times 10\,cm \times 100\,\mu s\,cm^{-1}$
$= 2000\,\mu s = 0.002\,s$

Frequency $= \dfrac{1}{T} = \dfrac{1}{0.002}$
$= 500\,Hz$

Amplitude $= 3.2\,cm \times 10\,V\,cm^{-1}$
$= 32\,V$

CRO adjustment

If there are too many waves being displayed across the screen, the time base setting needs adjustment. For example, a 50 Hz signal will give peaks which are 1 cm apart when the TB setting is $20\,ms\,cm^{-1}$. To increase the separation of the peaks to 2 cm, we would change the TB setting to $10\,ms\,cm^{-1}$.

Sometimes the tops of the peaks in the display are cut off. This requires adjustment of the gain control. Suppose the nominal peak is 5 cm high and the gain setting is $2\,V\,cm^{-1}$, then we are attempting to display a signal of 10 V in amplitude. If we want to reduce it to 2.5 cm, we simply double the gain setting to $4\,V\,cm^{-1}$.

> **Exam tip**
> Remember the time base controls the number of waves you see on the screen. The gain controls their height.

> **Knowledge check 54**
> You are asked to measure the frequency of a tuning fork using a CRO.
> a What additional apparatus is required?
> b How would you use the apparatus to find the frequency?

> **Exam tip**
> CROs are expensive pieces of equipment and it is unlikely that all centres have enough of them to allow their use in AS 3A or A2 3A. However, questions on CRO settings and the interpretation of CRO displays are certainly possible in AS 3B or A2 3B.

Questions & Answers

About this section

The AS 3B and A2 3B examination papers are designed to test your knowledge and understanding of physics practical techniques and procedures. They are both of 1-hour duration and both carry 50 marks. That means that you should spend not much more than 1 minute per mark in each question. In general, there are slightly more questions on the AS paper (usually 6) than there are in the A2 paper (usually 4). So the questions on the A2 3B paper are generally a little longer and are somewhat harder. They have what examiners call an element of 'stretch-and-challenge'.

The questions are all structured. That means each question is set around a theme, but there are many parts. In general, your answers will be quite short. They must be direct, relevant and focused on the material being assessed. While there are no QWC questions, it is important that your answers are coherent, written in good English and show an understanding of scientific vocabulary.

Both papers are synoptic. That means the AS paper contains material drawn from units AS 1 and AS 2. The A2 paper can contain material drawn from the AS course as well as the A2 course. In both papers, you are likely to see material which you have never encountered before. That should not be surprising. These are designed to be *skills-based* papers, so there is likely to be less material which is pure recall, that is, material which you just have to remember to get the right answer.

Question structure

The words of our physics teachers 'Read the question!' always ring in our ears. But you should do more than that. Many GCE questions have a set structure: a preamble, a command line and an advice line. It is helpful to recognise this structure when you are planning your response.

Consider the following question:

> A student is planning to investigate what property of light determines the width of the fringes produced by a given Young's double slit on a screen.
>
> Outline how you would carry out this investigation.
>
> You are not required to draw a diagram of the apparatus.

The first paragraph is the preamble – it sets the scene.

The second is called the command line – note carefully the command word 'Outline' which tells you the type of response the examiner requires.

The third line is the advice line – it gives you information about what the examiner expects.

Clearly, it is essential that you understand the meanings of the command words used in examination papers. In this case, it is essential that you know what is meant by the word 'outline'.

Command words

Calculate: Use a formula and carry out a calculation (usually with your calculator).

Choose: Select information from material that the question supplies.

Complete: Finish something that has already been started in the question, such as a table or a diagram.

Define: State formally the scientific meaning of a particular word or phrase.

Describe: Give a detailed account, in words, of relevant facts and features relating to the topic being examined.

Design: Use your knowledge and experience and be creative in solving an experimental task.

Determine: Use given data in a question to solve a problem.

Draw: Produce or add to some kind of illustration. This command requires you to take a little more time than that required to produce a 'sketch'.

Estimate: Use the numbers given in the question to produce an approximate answer to a problem.

Evaluate: Use the information supplied in the question, as well as any relevant outside knowledge, to consider evidence for and against an argument.

Explain: The answer must contain some element of reasoning or justification.

Give: Provide some new information.

Identify: Select key information from a source provided for you.

Justify: Use the evidence supplied to support and take one argument forward.

Label: Add text to a diagram, illustration or graph to indicate what particular items are.

Measure: Find a figure of data for a given quantity. You may also be asked to use an instrument to determine a particular property.

Name: Identify an object, an item, a process, a procedure or a theory.

Outline: This command word means 'summarise', but it is often used to ask students to set out how something should be done (such as 'Outline a plan', 'Outline an experiment' and so on).

Plan: Give detailed information about how a procedure or task might be carried out.

Plot: Draw and label axes on a grid and mark the points provided. If there is a correlation, you may also be asked to draw the line(s) of best fit. Remember that the line of best fit may be a curve.

Predict: Write down what you think will happen if a particular condition is met.

Show: Demonstrate with clear evidence that the statement given is true. You will often be expected to use the information provided.

State: This command word means the same as 'Write'.

Sketch: Produce some kind of illustration, which may be produced quickly.

Suggest: Use your knowledge and understanding to provide a solution to a problem you are unfamiliar with, or to explain an aspect of physics you may not have studied.

Use: Extract appropriate information from diagrams, tables or graphs etc. Remember that, if you do not show how you obtained this information, you will lose marks.

Write: Use written English in your answer. Unlike command words such as 'Design', 'Explain' or 'Describe', 'Write' usually only requires a short response.

Questions & Answers

AS 3B paper-style questions

Question 1

Figure 1 shows the readings on an ammeter and a voltmeter when used to find the resistance of a length of constantan wire.

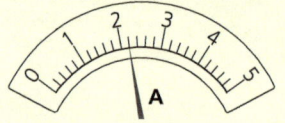 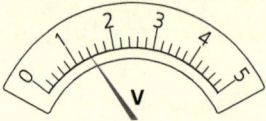

Figure 1

a State the reading on the ammeter shown in Figure 1. *1 mark*

> The first few questions of your examination paper are likely to be equally straightforward. But beware – there is no partial credit for a 1 mark question. You get full marks or you get zero marks.

b State the reading on the voltmeter shown in Figure 1. *1 mark*

c Calculate the percentage uncertainty in the ammeter reading. *2 marks*

> Always show your full working for all calculations. By doing so you may pick up marks for a correct method even if your final answer is incorrect.

The percentage uncertainty in the voltmeter reading is 7.1%.

d Calculate the absolute uncertainty in the resistance of the wire, giving your answer to 1 significant figure. *4 marks*

Student answer

a Ammeter reading = 2.2 A ✓

b Voltmeter reading = 1.4 V ✓

c Percentage uncertainty in the ammeter reading = $\frac{0.1}{2.2} \times 100\%$ ✓

= 4.5% ✓

d Resistance = $\frac{V}{I} = \frac{1.4\,V}{2.2\,A} = 0.64\,\Omega$ ✓

% uncertainty in resistance = % uncertainty in voltage + % uncertainty in current

= 7.1% + 4.5% = 11.6% ✓

Absolute uncertainty in resistance = 11.6% of 0.64 Ω ✓ = 0.074 Ω ✗

> In part d the student has not stated absolute uncertainty to 1 sf as required. The correct answer is 0.07 Ω (to 1 sf). Nonetheless, the first 3 marks are awarded because all the steps taken in the calculation are correct.
> **3/4 marks awarded**

AS 3B paper-style questions

Question 2

The resistance of a metal wire changes with temperature according to the equation:

$$R = R_0(1 + \alpha T)$$

where R_0 is the resistance at 0°C, T is the temperature in °C and α is a constant called the temperature coefficient of resistance.

The graphs in Figure 2 show the results of an experiment to investigate this relationship.

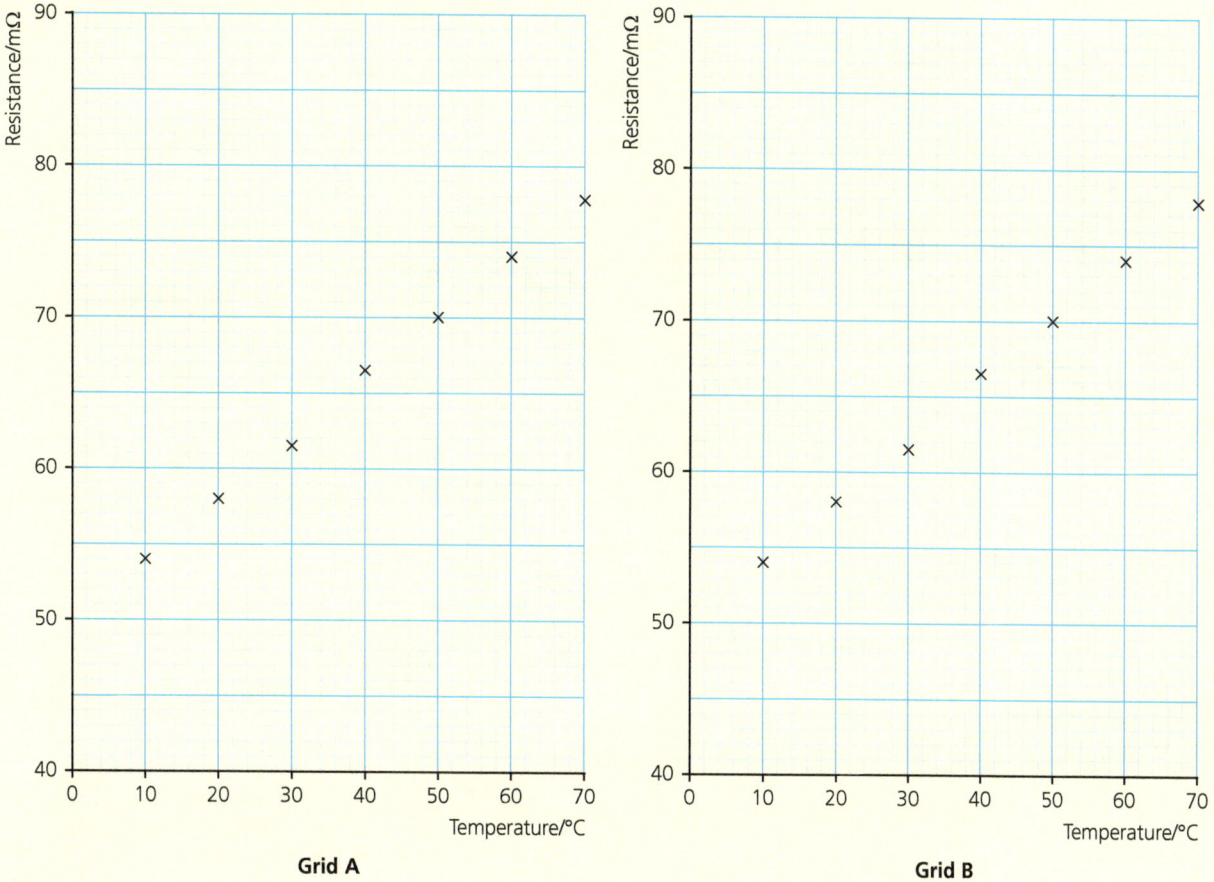

Figure 2

a On grid A, draw the line of best fit on the graph and use it to find the values of R_0 and α. State the units of α.

5 marks

b Estimate the % uncertainty in R_0 by drawing a line of extreme fit on grid B.

4 marks

Questions & Answers

Student answer

a

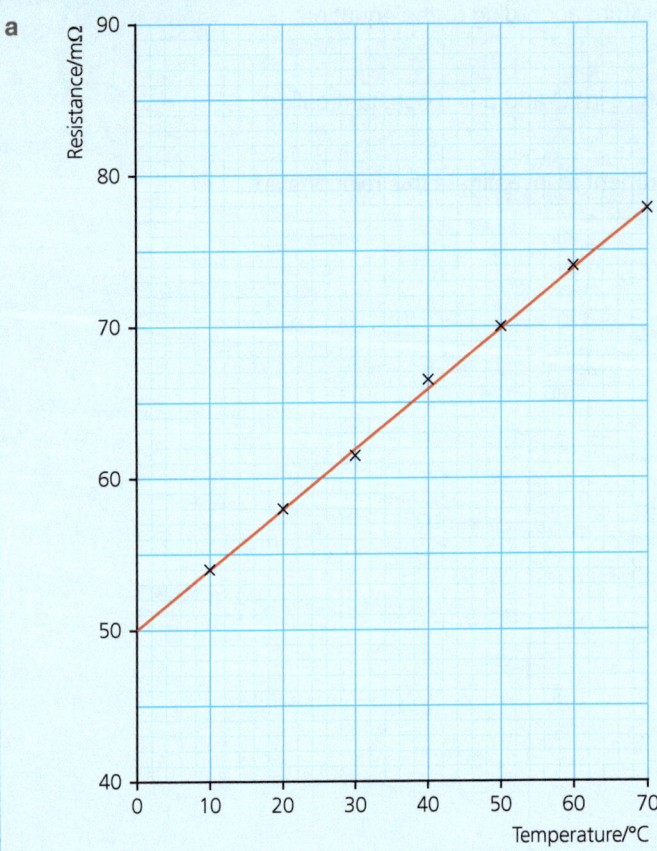

Grid A

Line of best fit ✓

Line of best fit shows R_0 as the intercept at 50 milliohms. ✓

Gradient = $R_0 \alpha = \dfrac{28\,\text{m}\Omega}{70\,°C} = 0.4\,\text{m}\Omega\,°C^{-1}$, ✓

so $\alpha = \dfrac{0.4\,\text{m}\Omega\,°C^{-1}}{50\,\text{m}\Omega} = 0.008\,°C^{-1}$ ✓ ✓ (number and unit)

> The student has shown as many points as possible on the line of best fit, with the same number of points just above and just below the line.
> **5/5 marks awarded**

b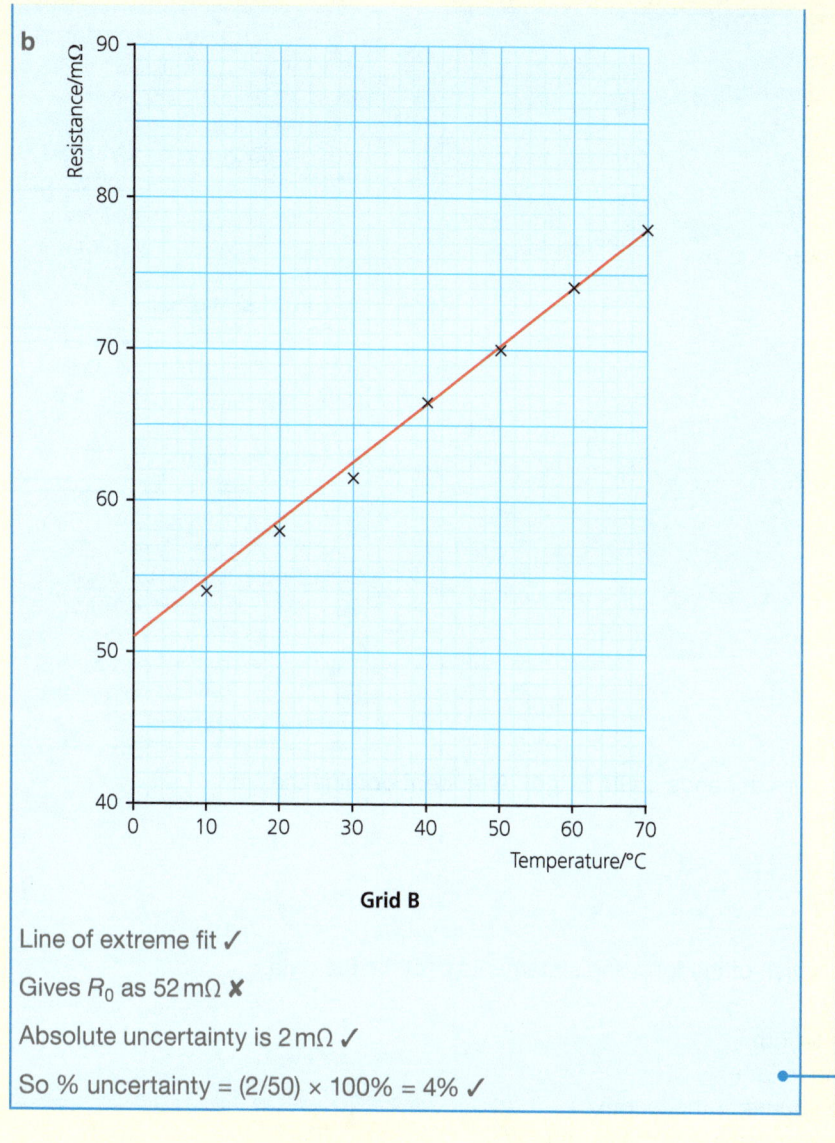

Grid B

Line of extreme fit ✓

Gives R_0 as 52 mΩ ✗

Absolute uncertainty is 2 mΩ ✓

So % uncertainty = (2/50) × 100% = 4% ✓

> The line of fit crosses the vertical axis one small square above 50 milliohms — but this corresponds to 51 mΩ, not 52 mΩ. The student would be penalised only once for this error. Note that an answer of 4% without showing the calculation would probably score only 1 mark — for the line of extreme fit. This example illustrates the necessity of showing the examiner exactly how you arrive at your answers.
> **3/4 marks awarded**

Question 3

The internal and external diameters of a glass tube were measured using callipers and found to be 6.3 ± 0.1 mm and 11.3 ± 0.1 mm.

a From these measurements, calculate the thickness of the tube, stating the absolute uncertainty in your answer. *2 marks*

b Calculate the % uncertainty in the thickness of the glass tube. *2 marks*

c Explain why the % uncertainty in the thickness of the glass is much bigger than that of the external diameter. *2 marks*

d Suggest, briefly, an alternative method to measure the thickness of the glass. *1 mark*

Questions & Answers

Student answer

a Thickness = $\frac{1}{2}$ × difference in diameters ✓

= 2.5 mm ± 0.1 mm ✓

> There are two common errors often made here. The first is to forget to halve the difference in the diameters; the second is to give the absolute uncertainty as ± 0.2 mm. **2/2 marks awarded**

b The % uncertainty = absolute uncertainty × $\frac{100\%}{\text{measured value}}$ ✓

= $\frac{0.1}{2.5}$ × 100% = 4% ✓

> Full marks here — but notice that any error in part a would have been carried forward into part b. **2/2 marks awarded**

c The absolute uncertainties add when determining the thickness ✓

But the thickness is very small, so % uncertainty is large ✓

> The student gets the key idea that the absolute uncertainty is a significant fraction of the thickness. **2/2 marks awarded**

d Use a lens to project a magnified image of end of tube on screen ✓
— divide thickness of image by the magnification.

> There are several possible responses here, all of which would gain credit. Examples are: mount tube horizontally and use a travelling microscope or a method based on volume of liquid displaced by the tube. Only 1 mark is being offered, so no detail is required. **1/1 mark awarded**

Question 4

The periodic time of a simple pendulum depends on its length. A student obtains the following data for such a pendulum:

Length L/cm	20	40	80
Periodic time T/s	0.90	1.27	1.80

a By inspecting the table, decide which of the following statements best fits the data.
The period is:

    A directly proportional to the length
    B inversely proportional to the length
    C directly proportional to the square of the length
    D directly proportional to the square root of the length

Justify your answer.   3 marks

b Describe how you could verify your choice by plotting a suitable straight-line graph.   2 marks

Student answer

a The period increases as L increases, so there is no inverse proportion: eliminates B ✓

does not increase by a factor of 1.5 when L does: not direct proportion, not A ✓

> The simple pendulum is not part of AS 1 or AS 2, but it can be assessed here because the examiner is seeking to test an experimental skill — interpretation of a set of results. The student's response is not quite complete. The student needs to explain why C can be eliminated or add that D doubles when L increases by a factor of 4, so D is confirmed. **2/3 marks awarded**

CCEA AS/A2 Physics Unit 3

b Plot the graph of T^2 against L ✓

> This response is not quite complete. The student needs to add that 'It should be a straight line through (0, 0)', confirming choice D. There are other equally acceptable responses, e.g. plot log T against log L – the relationship is confirmed if the line of best fit has a gradient of 0.5. However, this method would not be required of an AS student, but knowledge of it would be expected from an A2 student. **1/2 marks awarded**

Question 5

Figure 3 shows a potential divider circuit.

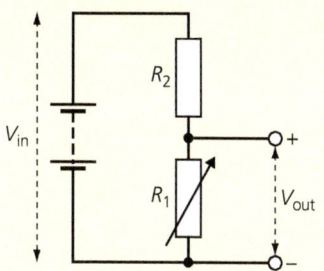

Figure 3

The output of the potential divider V_{out} is related to the input voltage V_{in} by the equation:

$$V_{out} = \frac{R_1 V_{in}}{R_1 + R_2}$$

a Show that $V_{out}^{-1} = V_{in}^{-1} + \frac{R_2}{R_1} \times V_{in}^{-1}$ 2 marks

A student obtains the following experimental results for this potential divider:

V_{out}/V	8.6	6.7	5.5	4.8	4.2
R_2/Ω	20	40	60	80	100
V_{out}^{-1}/V^{-1}					

b Plot a suitable straight-line graph from which the input voltage V_{in} and the unknown resistor R_1 might be found. You will first have to label and complete the blank row in the table. 6 marks

c Find the gradient of your graph and state its unit. 3 marks

d From the graph determine V_{in} and R_1. 4 marks

Student answer

a $V_{out} = \frac{R_1 V_{in}}{R_1 + R_2}$

$V_{out}^{-1} = \frac{R_1 + R_2}{R_1} \times V_{in}^{-1}$

$= (1 + \frac{R_2}{R_1}) \times V_{in}^{-1}$ ✓

Multiplying gives

$V_{out}^{-1} = V_{in}^{-1} + \frac{R_2}{R_1} \times V_{in}^{-1}$ ✓

> This is an excellent answer.
> **2/2 marks awarded**

b

V_{out}/V	8.6	6.7	5.5	4.8	4.2
R_2/Ω	20	40	60	80	100
V_{out}^{-1}/V^{-1}	0.12	0.15	0.18	0.21	0.24

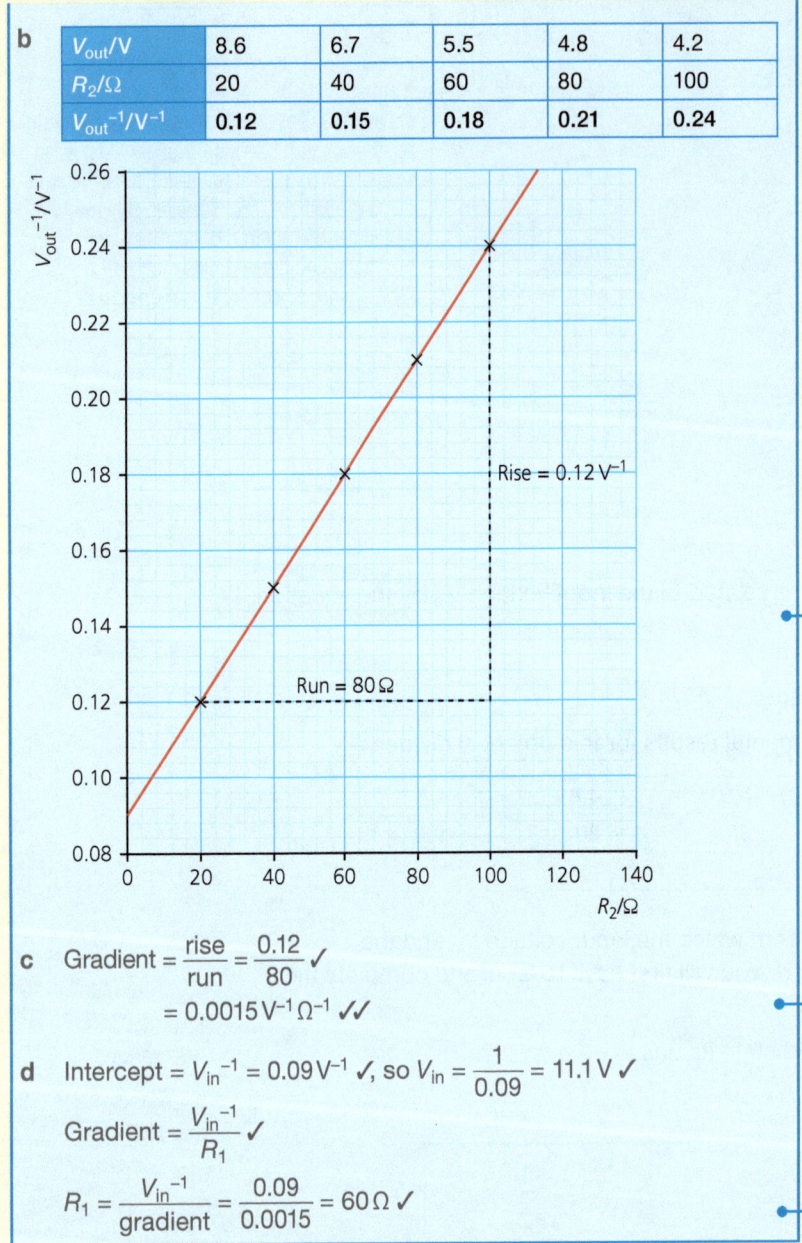

Values are all correctly calculated. Points all correctly plotted to within ±½ small square. Axis labels and units match exactly those in the table. Straight line of best fit drawn (with a ruler).
6/6 marks awarded

c Gradient = $\dfrac{\text{rise}}{\text{run}} = \dfrac{0.12}{80}$ ✓

= 0.0015 $V^{-1}\Omega^{-1}$ ✓✓

Correct numerical values for rise and run, correct calculation and unit. Note also that the triangle drawn on the grid is large. This is often referred to in CCEA mark schemes because small triangles inevitably lead to inaccurate values of gradients – an error of 1 Ω in a run of 80 Ω is insignificant, but the same error in a run of 5 Ω most certainly is. A small triangle would lead to a loss of 1 mark.
3/3 marks awarded

d Intercept = V_{in}^{-1} = 0.09 V^{-1} ✓, so $V_{in} = \dfrac{1}{0.09}$ = 11.1 V ✓

Gradient = $\dfrac{V_{in}^{-1}}{R_1}$ ✓

$R_1 = \dfrac{V_{in}^{-1}}{\text{gradient}} = \dfrac{0.09}{0.0015} = 60\,\Omega$ ✓

The student has correctly mapped the equation for V_{out}^{-1} to that of a straight line ($y = mx + c$) and shown the mapping in the answer. The student has also understood that R_1 is the intercept divided by the gradient. The arithmetic is accurate.
4/4 marks awarded

Question 6

A student sets up the circuit shown in Figure 4 and measures the terminal p.d. *V* on the voltmeter and the current *I* in the ammeter for different resistances *R*.

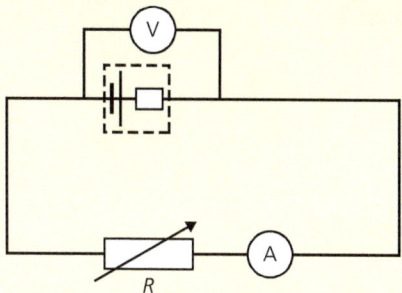

Figure 4

Using the apparatus in Figure 4, the student obtains the following data.

V/V	0.1	0.3	0.4	0.7	0.9	1.1	1.3
I/A	2.8	2.4	2.0	1.8	1.2	0.8	0.4

a In what way is the resistance of the rheostat changing as the reading on the voltmeter is increasing? Justify your answer. *2 marks*

b Describe how the output power of the cell is changing as the terminal p.d. increases from 0.1 V to 1.3 V. Justify your answer. *3 marks*

c How might the student determine the terminal p.d. at maximum power? *1 mark*

Student answer

a Resistance is increasing ✓

because current from battery is decreasing ✗

> Justification is incomplete. The student needs to indicate that resistance is the ratio $\frac{V}{I}$ and the ratio $\frac{V}{I}$ is increasing.
> **1/2 marks awarded**

b Output power $P = IV$ ✓

From the table, power is rising as voltage is rising ✗

> Inspection of the table shows product *IV* rises to some maximum value, and then falls — the maximum is between 0.7 V and 0.9 V. Student should have noticed the hint about power reaching a maximum in part c.
> **1/3 marks awarded**

c Take more voltage and current readings between 0.7 V and 0.9 V ✓

> Good experimental practice given in the answer. **1/1 mark awarded**

Questions & Answers

A2 3B paper-style questions

Question 1

Particles may be accelerated electrically using a potential difference V. The table shows how the speed of such particles v changes with V.

Potential difference/kV	60	80	100	120	140
Speed v/km s^{-1}	76.5	87.8	98.2	108	116
v^2/		5850		11 700	

a Copy the table and complete the row for v^2, giving the values to 3 sf. Two entries have been made for you. *4 marks*

b Plot the graph of v^2 (y-axis) against V (x-axis) and draw the line of best fit. *5 marks*

c Find the gradient of your line of best fit, giving your answer in m^2 s^{-2} V^{-1}. *6 marks*

d Show that m^2 s^{-2} V^{-1} is the same as C kg^{-1} and state the charge to mass ratio for the particle. *2 marks*

Student answer

a

Potential difference/kV	60	80	100	120	140
Speed v/km s^{-1}	76.5	87.8	98.2	108	116
v^2/km^2 s^{-2}	5850	7710	9640	11 700	13 500

A mark is awarded for the correct unit in the final row of the table. 1 mark is awarded for each of the correct values in the table, each reported to 3 sf (note that if these were reported to the wrong number of sf, these marks would be lost).
4/4 marks awarded

b

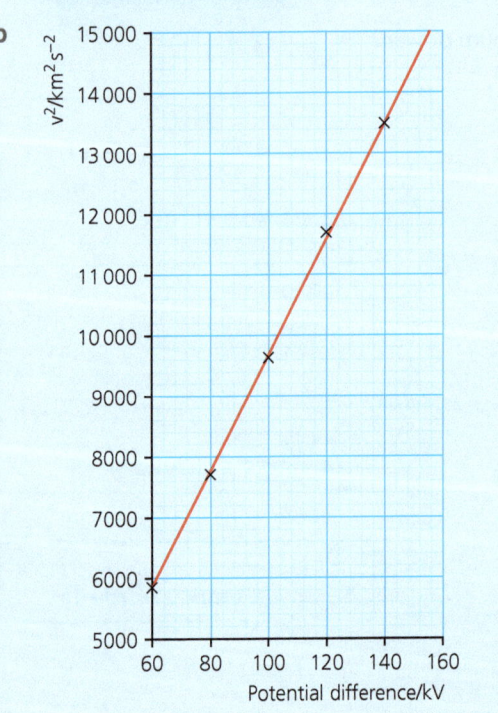

1 mark for both axis labels and units. 1 mark for suitable scale (covering at least ½ of each axis). 2 marks for points plotted on graph paper (1 mark if 3 points only are correctly plotted). 1 mark for line of best fit.
5/5 marks awarded

A2 3B paper-style questions

c gradient = $\frac{\text{rise}}{\text{run}}$ ✓

$= \frac{(13500 - 5580)}{(140 - 60)}$ ✗

$= 99 \text{ km}^2 \text{s}^{-2} \text{kV}^{-1}$ ✓

$1 \text{ km}^2 = 1000 \text{ m} \times 1000 \text{ m} = 1 \times 10^6 \text{ m}^2$ ✓

$1 \text{ kV}^{-1} = 1000 \text{ V}^{-1}$, so multiply by 1000 ✗

$99 \text{ km}^2 \text{s}^{-2} \text{kV}^{-1} = 99 \times 10^9 \text{ m}^2 \text{s}^{-2} \text{V}^{-1}$ ✓ ecf

> 1 mark for gradient formula. 0 mark for substitutions (the 5580 should have been 5850). 1 mark for gradient unit. 1 mark for conversion of km² to m². 0 mark for conversion of kV⁻¹ to V⁻¹ (1 kV = 1000 V so 1 kV⁻¹ = $\frac{1}{1000}$ V⁻¹ = 1×10^{-3} V⁻¹). 1 mark for final answer (error carried forward from conversion). Correct answer is $99 \times 10^3 \text{ m}^2 \text{s}^{-2} \text{V}^{-1}$.
> **4/6 marks awarded**

d $\text{m}^2 \text{s}^{-2} \text{V}^{-1} = \text{m}^2 \text{s}^{-2} (\text{JC}^{-1})^{-1} = \text{m}^2 \text{s}^{-2} \text{J}^{-1} \text{C} = \text{m}^2 \text{s}^{-2} (\text{kg m}^2 \text{s}^{-2})^{-1} \text{C}$
$= \text{m}^2 \text{s}^{-2} \text{kg}^{-1} \text{m}^{-2} \text{s}^2 \text{C} = \text{C kg}^{-1}$ ✓

since $qV = \tfrac{1}{2}mv^2$, gradient $= \frac{2q}{m}$, so $\frac{q}{m} = 4.95 \times 10^{10}$ C kg⁻¹ ✓ ecf

> Error carried forward from part c. Correct answer is 4.95×10^4 C kg⁻¹
> **2/2 marks awarded**

Question 2

A ball is dropped from a height h_0. The height h to which the ball rises after successive bounces n is thought to be given by the equation:

$$h = k^n h_0$$

where k is a constant.

In an investigation, the following experimental results were obtained:

n	2	3	4	5	6
h/cm	194	175	157	142	128

a i Express log h in terms of k, n and h_0.   1 mark

It is required to find the values of k and h_0 from the data.

    ii What linear graph should be plotted?   1 mark
    iii How might k and h_0 be found from such a graph?   4 marks

b Plot the graph and use it to find the values of k and h_0.   10 marks

You will find it helpful to use the blank row in the table.

> If you know you are going to have to find the gradient, choose the scale on the vertical axis with care and ensure the horizontal axis starts from 0. There is no time in the exam to plot the graph again.
>
> Look carefully at this student's response. It shows that all is not lost if the line does not cross the axis and the intercept is required. But the process is time consuming and unnecessary.
>
> It is worth reflecting a little before plotting the graph to find k. The ball cannot rise to a height greater than that from which it fell. That would contradict the principle of conservation of energy. Furthermore, k cannot be negative. A negative height would have no meaning. Both of these ideas tell us immediately that $0 < k < 1$.

Practical techniques and data analysis

Questions & Answers

Student answer

a **i** $\log h = n \times \log k + \log h_0$ ✓

> Correct application of theory of logs.
> **1/1 mark awarded**

   ii Plot $\log h$ on the vertical axis against n (horizontal axis). ✓

> **1/1 mark awarded**

   iii The gradient is $\log k$ ✓ and the intercept on the vertical axis is $\log h_0$ ✓

   So $k = 10^{\text{gradient}}$ ✓

   $h_0 = 10^{\text{intercept}}$ ✓

> **4/4 marks awarded**

b

n	2	3	4	5	6
h/cm	194	175	157	142	128
$\log (h/\text{cm})$	2.29	2.24	2.20	2.15	2.11

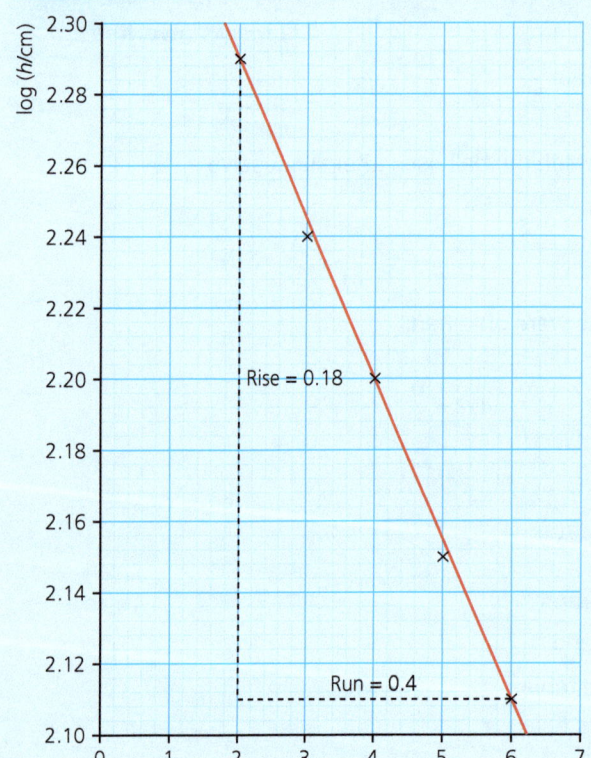

gradient $= \dfrac{\text{rise}}{\text{run}} = \dfrac{0.18}{4} = 0.045$

$k = 10^{\text{gradient}} = 1.11$

intercept cannot be found directly — so find equation of line

$\log h = -0.045 \times n + \text{intercept}$

substitute point (2, 2.29) into equation to get:

$2.29 = -0.045 \times 2 + \text{intercept}$

intercept $= 2.38$

$h_0 = 10^{\text{intercept}} = 10^{2.38} = 240 \, \text{cm}$

> Third row of table correctly labelled $\log (h/\text{cm})$ and not $\log h/\text{cm}$ which is the standard error — the h is measured in cm, the log itself has no unit. ✓ Values of $\log (h/\text{cm})$ inserted correctly into table. ✓✓ Axis labels and units both correct. ✓ Sensible scale chosen. ✓ Gradient – the student misses the fact that the gradient is negative – the correct answer is -0.045. ✗ Calculation of k – error carried forward – in fact $k = 10^{-0.045} = 0.90$ ✓ ecf (the student should have realised k must be less than 1 to conserve energy). Full 3 marks for obtaining h_0. ✓✓✓
> **9/10 marks awarded**

CCEA AS/A2 Physics Unit 3

A2 3B paper-style questions

Question 3

An investigation is carried out to determine the Young modulus of the material of a metal wire.

a What instrument would you use to find as accurately as possible the diameter of the wire? Justify your answer. *(3 marks)*

b Suggest two reasons why the diameter should be found several times and describe what should be done to obtain the value which is likely to be the most accurate value. *(2 marks)*

c What type of error is reduced by the process described in part b? *(1 mark)*

Student answer

a Micrometer screw gauge. ✓ The micrometer is suitable for a wide range of diameters ✓ (up to several cm) and has a resolution of 0.01 mm, so the diameters can be found with accuracy and precision. ✓

> The micrometer is the instrument of choice to find wire diameters and the reasons given are sound. **3/3 marks awarded**

b In the manufacturing process, the wire's bore may not have been made perfectly uniform. ✓ Measuring several different diameters of a given length of wire will confirm whether or not this is so.

> This is a comprehensive response. **2/2 marks awarded**

A single reading may be prone to error. Taking the mean of several different readings will reduce this error. ✓

c Systematic error. ✗

> The student has not understood the difference between random error and systematic error. **0/1 mark awarded**

Question 4

A steel sphere of radius a is placed near the edge of a watch glass of radius of curvature R and released. The sphere oscillates back and forth over the surface with a period T. An investigation is carried out to determine whether there is a relationship between T, a and R.

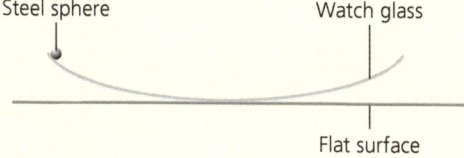

Figure 5

Theory suggests that the period T is given by: $T = 2\pi\sqrt{\dfrac{7(R-a)}{5g}}$. The time taken for the sphere to make one complete oscillation is a little under one second.

a Describe how you might accurately determine the period T of the oscillations. *(3 marks)*

b Map the equation given for the period to an equation of linear form. *(3 marks)*

c What graph would you plot to confirm the equation given for T? *(1 mark)*

d How would you use the graph to find R? *(2 marks)*

e How might the graph be used to find the acceleration of free fall g? *(2 marks)*

Questions & Answers

Student answer

a Measure the time T_{20} for a given sphere to make 20 oscillations over the watch glass. ✓ Repeat this timing of T_{20} twice more and calculate the mean value of T_{20}. ✓ The period T is the mean value of T_{20} divided by 20. ✓

> This is standard practice in timing experiments. In fact, it is usually the case that in this particular experiment friction reduces the maximum number of oscillations to about 10 or fewer. But the student is not expected to know that. Such information is gleaned only by carrying out some preliminary experimental work.
> **3/3 marks awarded**

b $T = 2\pi \sqrt{\dfrac{7(R-a)}{5g}}$

Squaring: $T^2 = 4\pi^2 \left[\dfrac{7(R-a)}{5g}\right]$ ✓

Expanding: $T^2 = \dfrac{28\pi^2}{5g} R - \dfrac{28\pi^2}{5g} a$ ✓

Compare with: $y = c + mx$ ✓

> A comprehensive response. The student has explained what mathematical process is being carried out on the LHS. This is unnecessary (and time-consuming) and not recommended, but it enables the reader to identify quickly if/where errors are made.
> **3/3 marks awarded**

c Plot T^2 against a. ✓

> The mapping clearly associates T^2 with y and a with x, so the question was straightforward for the student.
> **1/1 mark awarded**

d The intercept is $\dfrac{28\pi^2}{5g} R$ ✓

So, $R = \dfrac{5g}{28\pi^2}$ divided by the intercept. ✗

> The student has made a maths error. The term should be *multiplied* by the intercept. Setting out the work more clearly (as in part b) might have avoided this error. **1/2 marks awarded**

f The gradient is $-\dfrac{28\pi^2}{5g}$ ✓

So $g = \dfrac{28\pi^2}{5 \times \text{gradient}}$ ✓

> **2/2 marks awarded**

104 CCEA AS/A2 Physics Unit 3

Knowledge check answers

1. a $kg\,A^{-2}\,m^3\,s^{-3}$
   b $kg\,m^{-1}\,s^{-2}$
   c strain is dimensionless
   d $kg\,m^{-1}\,s^{-2}$

2. $5.3 \times 10^{-11}\,m$, $2.2 \times 10^7\,m\,s^{-1}$

3. a $\frac{1}{10}$
   b 30%
   c 7:3

4. $_an_w \times {_wn_g} \times {_gn_a} = 1$
   $1.33 \times {_wn_g} \times 0.667 = 1$
   $_wn_g$ = speed of light in water: speed of light in glass
   = 1.13

5. $\theta = \tan^{-1}(1.500) = 56.3° = 0.983$ radians

6. $R = \frac{V}{I} = \frac{2.55}{0.034} = 75\,\Omega$

7. a number like 4000

8. a $\sin i > \sin r$
   b $m_e \ll m_p$
   c $c_{\text{photon in air}} \approx c$

9. $A = \frac{P}{F}$ $g = \frac{k^2 L}{T^2}$ $R = \frac{(E-V)}{I}$ $\lambda = \frac{ay}{D}$ $x = \sqrt{(A^2 - \frac{v^2}{\omega^2})}$

10. a Plot V (vertical axis) against I (horizontal axis)
    b E = intercept on vertical axis, r = −gradient of the graph

11. a gradient = $\frac{\text{rise}}{\text{run}} = \frac{(20.0 - 5.5)\,m\,s^{-1}}{(6 - 0)\,s}$
       = $2.42\,m\,s^{-2} \approx 2.4\,m\,s^{-2}$
    b Gradient is decreasing as time increases

12. −10 (From theory of logs, $\ln(e^x) = x$, for all x)

13. Volume = area of annulus × length = $\pi(R^2 - r^2) \times L$
    = $\pi(0.75^2 - 0.6^2) \times 120 = 76.3\,cm^3$

14. Volume = $\frac{\text{mass}}{\text{density}} = \frac{1.66 \times 10^{-27}}{2.3 \times 10^{17}} = 7.22 \times 10^{-45}\,m^3$
    Volume $V = \frac{(4\pi r^3)}{3}$, so $r = \sqrt[3]{\frac{3v}{4\pi}} = \sqrt[3]{\frac{3 \times 7.22 \times 10^{-45}}{4\pi}}$
    = $1.20 \times 10^{-15}\,m$

15. a $\theta = 30° = \frac{\pi}{6}$ radians = 0.524 radians
    b $\theta = 60° = \frac{\pi}{3}$ radians = 1.047 radians
    c $\theta = 45° = \frac{\pi}{4}$ radians = 0.785 radians
    d $\theta = 0°$ (or 180°) = 0 radians (or π radians)

16. a $30° = \frac{\pi}{6}$ radians = 0.524 radians
    b $50° = 5\frac{\pi}{18} = 0.873$ radians
    c $60° = \frac{\pi}{3}$ radians = 1.047 radians
    d $80° = 4\frac{\pi}{9}$ radians = 1.396 radians

17. Angle sum = 180° = π radians = 3.142 radians

18. random error

19. a 0.3 mm
    b 7.5 − 0.3 = 7.2 mm

20. a 122.8 mm **or** 12.28 cm
    b 0.1 mm **or** 0.01 cm

21. There is only a small difference in the external and internal diameters of the pipe. So the thickness is quite small. The uncertainty in the diameter depends on the resolution of the callipers and is of the order of 0.1 mm. But this is of the same order of magnitude as the difference in the diameters, so the percentage uncertainty in the thickness will be high.

22. ACWM = CWM is expressly used in the principle of moments.
    The value of g cancels on each side of the equation.

23. a Plot h (vertical axis) against t^2 (horizontal axis)
    b Since $h = \frac{1}{2}gt^2$, the numerical value of g is twice the gradient of this graph.

24. The total mass of the accelerating system (trolley plus attached masses) must be kept constant.
    By transferring masses from the trolley to the hanger, the total mass remains the same, but the accelerating force is increased.

25. The product of the mass and the mean acceleration is, within the limits of experimental error, a constant, showing inverse proportion.

26. Attach masses to the glider (e.g. by using sticky tape) to increase the total mass and hence the momentum.

27. momentum $p = mv$, so unit for p is $kg \times m\,s^{-1} = kg\,m\,s^{-1}$
    $kg\,m\,s^{-1} = kg\,m\,s^{-2} \times s = N \times s = N\,s$

28. The greater the value of s, the smaller the percentage uncertainty in the loss of gravitational potential energy and the increase in kinetic energy.

29. a energy
    b charge; momentum

30. No. The resistance of a metal wire depends on its length, its cross-section area and the material from which it is made. Resistance is an intrinsic property of a material (like mass and volume). It still exists, even when the material is not conducting an electric current.

31. The voltage across the resistance wire is increased by reducing the resistance of the rheostat.

32. From the negative terminal of the battery towards the positive

33. Adding additional resistors draws more current from the battery. The total resistance of the circuit is the battery e.m.f. divided by the total current. Since the e.m.f. is constant, but the current drawn increases, the total resistance must decrease.

34. Copper (excellent conductor) has resistivity of order $10^{-8}\,\Omega\,m$
    Quartz (excellent insulator) has resistivity of order $10^{16}\,\Omega\,m$

35. A thermistor has a finite, non-zero resistance at all temperatures.
    Where the graph touches the vertical axis shows its resistance at 0 °C.

Knowledge check answers

Touching the horizontal axis would give the thermistor a resistance of zero at a particular temperature.

36 The cells each have an internal resistance of about $1\,\Omega$. So, the maximum current they could deliver is about 1.5 A, but the current required to start a car engine is around 100 A.

37 Refractive index n = speed of light in air/speed of light in glass

38 There is no bending because the incident ray is normal to the surface.
The angle of incidence is 0°.

39 To minimise experimental error. The possible lines between points which are close together, but in which there is an experimental error, have a high angular separation, which would lead to greater uncertainty in the position of the incident ray.

40 If the object is within the focal length, the image is virtual. So no image could be produced on the screen.

41 At the point where the straight line $u = v$ crosses the curve, the object and image distances are the same. This happens only when $u = v = 2f$. So, the coordinates of P are $(2f, 2f)$.

42 a Independent: v; dependent: M; control: f
   b Random — sometimes the value of v will be too large, sometimes too small
   c Each student in the group determines v independently and the mean value is found.

43 a In a stationary wave, all particles between two adjacent nodes are in the same phase.
     In a progressive wave, all particles within a given wavelength have different phase.
   b half a wavelength ($\lambda/2$)

44 It is important to start at zero in case the fundamental resonance frequency at a given length is lower than the starting frequency. The frequency is increased slowly to ensure that fundamental resonance is detected. (There are resonances at higher frequencies and these are to be avoided.)

45 To improve the contrast and hence the visibility of the fringes.

46 As the grating element decreases, each maximum becomes narrower and has greater intensity and the separation of the maxima increases.

47 Steel is strong in tension. Reinforcing steel rods make the concrete stronger in tension.

48 To control the voltage and current in the immersion heater and hence its output power.

49 $T = 2\pi\sqrt{\dfrac{l}{g}} = 2\pi\sqrt{\dfrac{0.25}{1.6}} = 2.48\,\text{s}$

$f = \dfrac{1}{T} = \dfrac{1}{2.48} = 0.40\,\text{Hz}$

50 The motion of a simple pendulum is not one at constant acceleration.

51 At the highest point in the motion, the spring has maximum compression; at the lowest point, the spring has maximum extension.

52 After 1 time constant, percentage fall = $e^{-1} \times 100\%$
   = 36.8%
   After 2 time constants, percentage fall = $e^{-2} \times 100\%$
   = 13.5%
   After 3 time constants, percentage fall = $e^{-3} \times 100\%$
   = 5.0%

53 After 1 time constant, percentage of battery e.m.f. reached = $(1 - e^{-1}) \times 100\% = 63.2\%$
   After 2 time constants, percentage of battery e.m.f. reached = $(1 - e^{-2}) \times 100\% = 86.5\%$
   After 3 time constants, percentage of battery e.m.f. reached = $(1 - e^{-3}) \times 100\% = 95.0\%$

54 a microphone
   b Connect microphone leads to CRO input terminals and switch on the time base.
     Sound the tuning fork over the microphone and adjust the TB and sensitivity (gain) control until a sinusoidal wave is observed on the screen.
     Measure the mean distance between the peaks on the screen using the graticule.
     Convert this distance to a time T using the time base setting.
     The frequency of the fork f is calculated using $f = \dfrac{1}{T}$.

Index

Note: **bold** page numbers indicate key term definitions.

A

absolute uncertainty 28, 29–30, 66
acceleration
   common and derived unit for 8
   Newton's second law 41–44
acceleration of free fall 38–41
   energy conservation experiment 46–48
accuracy **25**
algebra 11–13
   changing the subject of an equation 12–13
   symbols 11–12
amplitude
   electrical signals 88–89
   simple pendulum 81–82
analysis 26–30
   measurement limitations 27–30
   observations, making and recording 27
angle of incidence **60**
angle of refraction **60**
apparatus for practicals 24–25
area
   common and derived unit 8
   formulae for calculating 20, 22
   surface area 20
   under graphs, finding 16–17
arithmetic mean **11**
arithmetic and numerical computation 7–10

B

base units **7**
battery, e.m.f. and internal resistance of 58–59

C

capacitance calculation 87
capacitor discharge and charge 84–87
cathode ray oscilloscope (CRO), voltage and frequency 88–89
centre of gravity (CoG) of an object 35
charge of a capacitor 84–87
circumference, calculating 20
coherent **71**
collisions, conservation of linear momentum 44–46
combined uncertainties 30
communication 31
conservation
   of energy 46–48
   of linear momentum in a collision 44–46
control variables **25**
converging lens, focal length of 64–66
critical angle **63**
   of glass or Perspex®, measurement of 63–64
CRO (cathode ray oscilloscope) 88–89

D

data handling 10–11
dataloggers 26
decimal vs standard form 8
density of a solid or liquid 33–35
dependent variable **25**
derived units **8**
diffraction grating, wavelength of light experiment 73–75
directly proportional **15**
discharge of a capacitor 84–87
double-slit experiment, wavelength of light 71–73

E

electrical signals, determining frequency and amplitude of 88–89
e.m.f. (electromotive force) of a battery 58–59, 85–86
energy
   common and derived units 8
   conservation 46–48
equations, rearranging 12–13, 14
errors 27–28
estimation 10
evaluation of experiments 30–31
experimental data, uncertainty in 66
exponentials 9, 20

F

falling body experiments
   acceleration of free fall 38–41
   energy conservation 46–48
filament lamp, I–V characteristic of 50–51
focal length of a converging lens 64–66
force(s)
   calculating unknown 35
   common and derived units 8
   Newton's second law 41–44
   tensile 76, 77
   using trigonometrical functions 21–22
fractions 9
frequency
   cathode ray oscilloscope (CRO) measuring 88–89
   common and derived units 8
   sound waves 69–70

G

gain control, CRO 88–89
geometry 20
glass
   determining critical angle of 63–64
   refraction and Snell's law 60–62
gradient
   of a curve 15–16
   of a straight-line graph 15
graphs 13–20
   area under 16–17
   gradient as rate of change 15–16
   gradient of straight-line graph 15
   logarithmic plots 17–19
   of motion, mapping to straight-line 14–15
   sketching of functions 19–20
   straight-line graphs 13–15

Index

grating, diffraction 73–75
gravitational potential energy 46–47, 48

I
implementing 24–26
  accuracy and precision 25–26
  dataloggers 26
  outline plans 24–25
  variables 25
independent variable **25**
index 10
intercept of a straight-line graph 13
internal resistance of a battery 58–59
inversely proportional **41**
I–V characteristic
  of a filament lamp 50–51
  of a metal wire 50

K
kinetic energy 46–48

L
lens equation for real images
  using to show magnification ratio 67–68
  verifying experimentally 64–66
light
  determining wavelength of 71–75
  refraction of 60
light gates, using 38–40, 42, 43, 45, 47–48
linear momentum, conservation of in a collision 44–46
liquids
  density of 29–30, 33–35
  specific heat capacity of 78–80
loaded spiral spring oscillations 82–84
logarithmic plots 17–19

M
magnification of a real image 66–68
mass
  and acceleration, Newton's second law 41–44

density calculation 33–35
finding value of unknown 35–38
mathematics 7–22
  algebra 11–13
  arithmetic and numerical computation 7–10
  data handling 10–11
  geometry and trigonometry 20–22
  graphs 13–20
mean **11**
measurement limitations 27–30
  errors, dealing with 27–28
  uncertainty 28–30
moments of forces 35–38
momentum, conservation of 44–46
monochromatic light **71**
  diffraction of 74
multimeter, using 48–49, 51–52
multiples **8**

N
natural logarithms 9–10, 18–19
negative temperature coefficient (ntc) thermistor 55–57
Newton's second law, verifying mathematically 41–44
newton, unit of force 8, 41
normal 60

O
observations, making and recording 27
ohmmeter, determining resistance using 48–49
optical density 60
orders of magnitude 10
oscillations
  of a loaded spiral spring 82–84
  of a simple pendulum 80–82
oscilloscope, using 88–89
outlier **44**
outline plans 24–25

P
parallel resistors 51–53
pendulum, motion of simple harmonic 80–82
percentages 9
percentage uncertainty 29–30
planning experiments 24
plots *see* graphs
potential difference *see* voltage
powers and uncertainty 30
practical activities 32–89
  acceleration of free fall 38–41
  capacitor discharge and charge 84–87
  cathode ray oscilloscope (CRO) 88–89
  conservation of linear momentum in a collision 44–46
  critical angle measurement 63–64
  density of a solid or liquid 33–35
  e.m.f. and internal resistance of a battery 58–59
  energy exchange between potential and kinetic for a falling body 46–48
  focal length of a converging lens 64–66
  magnification of a real image 66–68
  mass of a ruler, finding 36–38
  motion of the simple pendulum 80–82
  negative temperature coefficient (ntc) thermistor 55–57
  Newton's second law, verifying mathematically 41–44
  oscillations in a loaded spiral spring 82–84
  resistance determination 48–51
  resistivity of a material 53–55
  resistors in series and parallel 51–53
  Snell's law and refractive index 60–62
  specific heat capacity 78–80
  speed of sound in air 69–70
  unknown mass, finding 36

Index

wavelength of light 71–75
Young modulus 76–78
practical skills 23–31
  analysis 26–30
  communication 31
  evaluation 30–31
  implementing 24–26
  refinement 31
precision **26**
prefixes 8
principle of moments (PoM) 35–38
Pythagoras' theorem 21

R
radians 9, 22
random errors 27–28, **31**
real images
  lens equation for 64–66
  magnification of 66–68
refinement 31
refractive index **60**, 61–62
relative uncertainty 29–30
reliability **31**
repeatable **42**
resistance
  ammeter–voltmeter method of finding 48–50
  common and derived units 8
  internal resistance of a battery 58–59
  ntc thermistor experiment 55–57
  of resistors in series and parallel 51–53
resistivity of a material 53–55
resolution **26**
  and measurement uncertainty 28–29
right-angled triangles
  gradient of 16
  Pythagoras' theorem 21
  trigonometrical functions 21

S
semicircular block, critical angle of glass 63–64
series resistors 51–53
shapes, equations for area, volume and circumference 20
signal generator (oscillator) 69, 88
significant figures **11**
simple functions, sketching 19–20
simple harmonic motion
  of loaded spiral spring 82–84
  of simple pendulum 80–82
SI system (Système Internationale) **7**
slope of a graph *see* gradient
Snell's law, verifying 60–62
solid, determining density of 33–34
solidus notation 27
sound, determining speed of in air 69–70
specific heat capacity
  common and derived units 8
  electrical method for determining 78–80
speed
  calculation example 12
  common and derived units 8
  of sound in air 69–70
spring oscillation 82–84
standard form **8**
stationary waves 69
straight-line graphs 13–15
  gradient of 15–16
  simple mappings 14–15
strain 76–78
stress 76–78
submultiples **8**
surface area, calculating 20
symbols, algebraic 11–12
systematic errors 28, **31**

T
tables, recording data in 27
temperature
  and resistance 48–51, 55–57
  specific heat capacity 78–80
tensile force 76, 77
thermistors 55–57
time base (TB) control, CROs 88–89
time constant, charging and discharging capacitor 84–87
total internal reflection 63, 64
trigonometry
  calculations 20
  defining sine, cosine and tangent 21
  degrees and radians 9, 22
  Pythagoras' theorem 21
  ratios ($\sin x$, $\cos x$ and $\tan x$) 9

U
uncertainty (in measurement) **28**
  absolute and relative 29–30
  calculations 34
  combined 30
  in the experimental data 66
  other factors affecting 28–29
  and powers 30
uniform metre ruler, finding mass of 36–37
units
  changing from one to another 8
  international system of 7–8
unknown mass, finding 35–36

V
variables 25
voltage
  across a capacitor 85–87
  cathode ray oscilloscope 88–89
  common and derived units 8
  and electrical resistance 48–51
  ntc thermistor experiment 56
volume
  calculating 20
  common and derived units 8

W
wavelength of light
  diffraction grating experiment 73–75
  double slit experiment 71–73

Y
Young modulus for material of a metal wire 76–78